Collins

English for Business

WRITING

Nick Brieger

HarperCollins Publishers
The News Building
1 London Bridge Street
London SE1 9GF

First edition 2011
Latest Reprinted Indian edition 2016

Reprint 10 9 8 7 6 5 4 3 2 1 0

ISBN 978–93–5177–303–0

www.collinselt.com
www.collins.in

A catalogue record for this book is available
from the British Library

Typeset by Davidson Publishing Solutions, Glasgow

Printed in India by Replika Press Pvt. Ltd.

About the author

After a first degree in Law and an M.A. in Applied Linguistics, **Nick Brieger**'s early career included language training and teacher training in Eastern and Western Europe. In the 80s, he worked with teachers and trainers on developing communication skills programmes for managers in Poland, Hungary, Russia, Ukraine and Georgia. In the 90s, as the focus for global business moved towards Asia, he worked on programmes to develop English language competence for those wishing to follow an international career. In recent years, he has worked with a range of major public and private international organisations on communication, team building and intercultural training programmes. In addition to his training activities, he is the author of more than 20 books in the field of language, communication and culture.

Contents

Introduction 2

Section 1 – Who are my readers?

Unit 1	Choosing the correct amount of information	4
Unit 2	Choosing the right technical level	8
Unit 3	Planning the document	12

Section 2 – What structure and organisation for my document?

Unit 4	Layout for an email or letter	16
Unit 5	Linking 1: Connecting sentences	20
Unit 6	Linking 2: Sentence structure	24

Section 3 – What tone for my readers?

Unit 7	Recognising and using tone	28
Unit 8	Varying tone with words and expressions	32
Unit 9	Varying tone using sentence structure and sentence length	36

Section 4 – What language for my document?

Unit 10	Starting off: Greeting, introduction and reference	40
Unit 11	The main part: Signalling intentions	44
Unit 12	Finishing off: Next steps, pre-closing and farewell	48

Section 5 – How do I write efficiently?

Unit 13	Writing clearly and simply	52
Unit 14	Writing transparently	56
Unit 15	Writing quickly	60
Unit 16	Editing for accuracy: Checking and correcting language	64

Section 6 – How do I put it all together?

Unit 17	Best practice 1: Emails	68
Unit 18	Best practice 2: Business reports	72
Unit 19	Best practice 3: Minutes	76
Unit 20	Best practice 4: Business writing	80

Appendix 1	Key phrases for business letters and emails	84
Appendix 2	Linking words and phrases	88
Appendix 3	Reporting verbs	89
Appendix 4	Sample documents	90

Glossary 102

Answer key 110

Introduction

Collins English for Business: Writing will help you to write more effective business documents in a more efficient way.

You can use *Writing*:

- as a self-study course
- as supplementary material on a business communication or business English course.

Writing will help you develop your **knowledge of** and **skills in** business writing. The book is divided into two main parts:

1 the elements of an **effective document**

2 the process of **efficient writing**

The starting point for the first part is a framework to introduce the core elements of effective documents: emails, reports, and minutes of a meeting. The second part helps you become more efficient by writing more clearly, more simply and more quickly.

Writing contains 20 units. These are arranged into six sections.

1 Who are my readers?

2 What structure and organisation for my document?

3 What tone for my readers?

4 What language for my document?

5 How do I write efficiently?

6 How do I put it all together?

At the back of the book there are:

- the Appendices
- a Glossary – this highlights the most difficult words from each unit giving definitions and further examples from the Collins COBUILD Advanced Dictionary
- the Answer key – providing model answers to the exercises

Unit structure

Each of the 20 units of *Writing* focuses on a separate feature of business writing. In order to develop your knowledge and skills, each unit provides:

- an introduction to the writing feature, explaining and demonstrating its relevance to business writing
- tasks to practise the specific feature of business writing.

In order to increase awareness of the international dimension of communication, each unit includes a short **cultural note**. This is intended to encourage reflection on the impact of culture on your business writing.

Using *Writing*

There are three ways to use this book:

1 Work through the units from 1–20

2 Choose from the Contents page (as trainer or learner) those units which correspond with your specific learning needs

3 Refer to Unit 20 to assess your personal learning needs

Study tips

For ease of use, each unit follows the same structure. It is recommended that you follow these steps when working though a unit:

- read through the first section which explains the writing feature and demonstrates its relevance to business writing
- work through the practice tasks
- compare your answers with the key
- regularly revise and go over what you have learnt

Language level

Writing has been written to help business learners at B2 level and above (Upper Intermediate to Advanced).

Other titles

Also available in the *Collins English for Business* series: *Listening* and *Speaking*.

1 Choosing the correct amount of information

I'm sorry I wrote you such a long letter; I didn't have time to write a short one. – Blaise Pascal (French theologist and mathematician)

The first step in writing a document is choosing the content. To do this effectively, ask yourself the following questions:

1 How much information does the reader actually need?

2 If you are asking for information, is your request concise so that the reader knows how to reply?

3 If you are giving information, is your message precise and easy to understand?

Using **correct language** is only a small part of effective writing; you need to think about the **appropriate information** for your document.

When writing professional documents, it is easy to include more information than is required. For example, when a specialist communicates with a non-specialist, the specialist may overestimate how much the non-specialist needs to know; or perhaps the specialist wants to show their expertise by giving a very full answer to a question, when a brief response would be better. Therefore it is important to spend time on **planning** the content of your writing before you start and **editing** the content of your document after you have written the first draft.

As a skill, writing requires more planning (before) and editing (after) than speaking. When you speak, you can check your listener's understanding by the feedback you receive. When you write, this feedback is less immediate, as it takes time for written communication to be exchanged.

Finally, we live in a world with easy access to enormous quantities of data. Make your readers' lives easier by converting the **data** into usable and useful **information**.

Useful tips

Planning	Editing
• What does my reader already know about this subject? • How much information do they need to know? • How can I present the information in a concise way so that it is easy to understand?	• Is there too much or too little detail for my reader? • Is there any redundant information, e.g. repetition? • Are there any gaps in the information which will make it difficult for the reader to understand?

1 **Whether a document contains redundant information will depend on:**

1 the writer's view of how much information the reader needs

2 the reader's view of their actual needs in terms of information

However, to encourage you to think about the right quantity of information for your reader, here are some expressions which give examples of redundant language. In each phrase, put brackets around the redundant word(s).

1 advance planning
2 advance reservations
3 all meet together
4 basic fundamentals
5 cheap price
6 close proximity
7 difficult challenge
8 each and every
9 end result
10 estimated roughly at
11 general public
12 past experience
13 reason is because
14 regular routine
15 unexpected surprise

2 **Read through the following email written by a computer maintenance company about a customer's problem with their computer monitor. In the email, find the following:**

a three examples of redundant information. Cross these out.

b two examples of missing information. Put asterisks where this information should be.

To: jknowles@knowles.com

Subject: Returns

Your reference: monitor XT3458

Dear customer

We have received your request to return the faulty monitor, which is not displaying the correct colours. We will process this as fast as possible. In order to provide a quick and reliable service, we kindly ask you to follow these instructions closely:

Within the next twelve hours, you will receive two emails from GTS. In the first email you will find a link to a GTS return label. Please print out this label with a laser printer. With this number you can track the delivery status of your item on the Internet.

Please pack your defective device into its original packaging. Afterwards please stick the return label clearly onto the box so that it is easily visible. When your parcel is ready for collection, please call GTS to arrange for collection.

Make sure you pack your defective device in the original packaging! If you don't have the original packaging or any other secure packaging for transportation, contact us by email so that we can provide you with suitable packaging. Please let us know.

Please only send in your defective LCD display together with its stand and the external power adapter (without its power cord). You will be charged for extra shipping costs in case we need to send back any accessories which you sent to us in error.

Yours sincerely
Electronic Computer Services

3 **Read the two job-related emails:**

a an email for a job in sales and marketing

b an email for an internship.

Look at the quantity of information in each document and decide if there is too much or too little.

a

To: seansmith@autosales.com
Subject: Application

Dear Mr Smith

I am responding to your advertisement in *The Daily Observer* of 8 January 2011, regarding the Automotive Sales Representative position. Attached is my CV, showing my education, experience, and background.

As you will see from my CV, I graduated from the University of Watersville in 2007 with an upper second class honours degree in Business Administration. During my final year I was attracted to the areas of sales and marketing, and followed a three-term specialist course, which focused on:

- Fundamentals of Marketing
- Business Communications
- Fundamentals of Customer Care
- Managing Marketing Information Systems
- Promotional Practice
- Sales & Marketing Operations
- Promotional Practice Management
- Marketing Communication Strategy

My CV lists the jobs that I have held. As you will see, I worked as a trainee in the marketing department of Custom Visuals for two years (2007–2009), where I learned about advertising and organising promotional events. I was then promoted to the position of marketing executive, where I worked on planning and implementing advertising campaigns. However, after one year in that position, I decided to move to Q Cars, where I managed key accounts, especially in the area of car leasing. I learned a considerable amount about planning and organising events. After two years at Q Cars, I decided to move on and found a position as marketing manager for SpecTex, a specialist textile company. There I headed up a small sales team, as well as having responsibility for marketing activities in terms of product distribution. Throughout my sales and marketing career I have won top sales awards, and, in my last job, was involved in training other sales representatives in specific sales techniques to increase their sales. I hope my application will be of interest to you. I am available to come in for interview at a mutually convenient time. I look forward to hearing from you.

Yours sincerely

Mary Green

b

To: jenbryant@nt.ac.uk

Subject: internship

Dear Ms Bryant

I am interested in applying for the scientific research internship that I recently saw advertised in the University Career Services Office.

I have had lots of laboratory experience in chemistry, biology, and geology. So, I feel I would be a suitable candidate. And last summer, I worked as an assistant for a small pharmaceutical company near my home.

I hope you find my application of interest.

Yours sincerely

Sarah Bentley

4 **Look at the two emails again and list the information that you think should be included. Then rewrite them.**

Email a	**Email b**
•	•
•	•
•	•

Cultural note

The quantity of information that you may find in communication, including written documents, is not the same for all national cultures. The major difference is between **low context cultures** and **high context cultures**.

In low context cultures, people typically expect information to be made explicit in their communication and can comfortably manage large quantities of data. Words are typically used to transmit information and data.

In high context cultures, on the other hand, background information tends to be implicit and assumed to be shared. Words are used in a more indirect way, leaving the reader to work out for themselves the full significance of the message from the context.

2 Choosing the right technical level

When something can be read without effort, great effort has gone into its writing. – Enrique Jardiel Poncela (Spanish playwright and novelist)

Technical level refers both to information and to language. Choosing the right technical level for your readers means standing back from both your technical expertise and your technical language, and putting yourself into your readers' shoes. When you do that, you can start to pitch your writing at an appropriate technical level for your reader.

The 'silo effect' is a phrase that is often used to describe the failure of communication in business communities. What does it mean?

A silo is a storage building for grain. It has no windows so people working inside one silo cannot see others – either people inside other silos in their own organisation or outside.

Within a silo, people speak the same language and understand each other comfortably. They have developed a shared specialist code of language using acronyms (WAH – working at home; MSRP – Manufacturer's Suggested Retail Price), abbreviations (ch. ppd. – charges prepaid; biz dev – business development), technical forms, and shortcuts to meanings. However, when they are asked to communicate outside their silo, they lack the sensitivity to adapt their communication so that other people understand them without effort.

Therefore, to be understood without effort, communication requires:

- a sensitivity to your readers
- an understanding of their technical level
- an awareness of how much information they need
- a 'bridge' to their communicative world.

'Gobbledygook'

The term 'gobbledygook' was invented by former US Representative Maury Maverick to describe any text containing jargon or complex language which makes it unnecessarily hard to understand.

The Plain English Campaign encourages writers to avoid the use of jargon as it makes the reader feel inferior, frustrated, and angry, and causes a divide between the writer and the reader.

Useful tips

Do	Don't
• ask yourself what your readers already know about the subject • write at an appropriate technical level for your readers • be specific, concrete; give examples • remember to edit your writing to check for comfortable understanding	• use jargon from your silo • use abbreviations unless you know your readers understand them • include technical detail that is beyond the knowledge of your readers • write in complex language (vocabulary, sentence length, sentence structure) that makes the meaning difficult to understand • use abstract ideas when concrete facts would be easier to understand

Here are some examples of over-complex writing. First, we have used the **Don't** list from the **Useful tips** box to identify the reasons why it is so difficult to understand, and then we have suggested improvements.

1a From an education policy document:

Before improvement

High-quality learning environments are a necessary precondition for facilitation and enhancement of the ongoing learning process.

Why is it difficult to understand?

- Abstract idea
- Complex vocabulary

After improvement

Children need good schools if they are to learn properly.

2b From a legal contract between a lender and borrower:

Before improvement

All transactions effected pursuant to this instrument shall be effected for the account and risk and in the name of the undersigned; and the undersigned hereby agrees to indemnify and hold you harmless from, and to pay you promptly on demand, any and all losses arising therefrom or any debit balance due thereon.

Why is it difficult to understand?

- Complex vocabulary
- Long sentences
- Complicated sentence structure

After improvement

You will be responsible for anything you owe on your account.

3c From a healthcare policy document:

Before improvement

The aim of this resource pack is to help organisations promote and implement the use of an HR Leadership Qualities Framework that describes those behaviours which enhance HR capacity and capability to improve the patient experience.

Why is it difficult to understand?

- Complex vocabulary
- Technical detail

After improvement

This resource pack will help organisations promote and introduce a Human Resources Leadership Qualities Framework. The framework will help HR departments to improve the experience of patients.

Now use the *Don't* list from the *Useful tips* box to identify the main reasons why the following paragraphs are difficult to understand. Then try to rewrite them so that they are easier to understand. The first two require only small changes, while the last two need more major work.

1 From a letter of application for a job:

During three years at XYZ and four years at ABC I built up a broad fundamental knowledge of food science and processing. My desire to extend my contribution through to product completion necessitated that I provide a communication interface between the scientifically focused, laboratory-based personnel and the process-driven pilot plant research groups. In the international working environments offered by XYZ and ABC, I gained the necessary interpersonal skills to exclude cultural and scientific misunderstandings, and employed fully my linguistic skills to ensure optimal project results and sociable working relations.

2 From a policy statement:

This year we have reviewed our quality improvement plan to focus on and cross-reference to the new Blueprint For Excellence so we are working towards fulfilling future expectations enabling a more workable and live document which will meet with the approval of the BGDF.

3 From the promotional material for a new IT product:

We are pleased to announce our new, easy to use and improved cutting-edge technology leverages innovative, robust and high-performance outcomes while uniquely positioning us to focus on world-class partnerships. Next generation outcomes are easily scalable and flexible up to 120 percent.

4 From a contract for transportation of goods:

The Carrier shall not be liable for injury or damage to or destruction or loss of the Goods or any other property arising out of or incidental to or in connection with or occurring during the provision of the Services or for the mis-delivery or non-delivery of the Goods and whether or not caused or contributed to by the default (including negligence) of the Carrier or any agent, servant or officer of the Carrier or any other person entitled to the benefit of these conditions.

Cultural note

Not all cultures place the same value on **simplicity**. In some contexts, simplicity may be seen as a lack of professionalism or true understanding of the subject. Simple language may also be judged as simplistic language and may be seen as a lack of competence.

It is important, therefore, to put your writing into the cultural context of your readers so that you can choose the appropriate technical level. Too complex and your writing may remain unread because it is too difficult; too simple and your writing may be ignored because it is not demanding enough.

3 Planning the document

If you don't know where you are going, any road will get you there.
– Lewis Carroll (English author)

The four-box document plan

1 Purpose (15-second rule)

- key message
- arouse interest
- use key words to give right feeling

2 Background or explanation

- give background, if necessary
- reinforce or explain your key message
- arrange ideas

3 Details

- keep this section as short as possible
- move supporting material to an appendix

4 What next?

- summarise main ideas
- use powerful idea to end
- state who is going to do what, and when

The four-box document plan is a tool to help you organise the content of your document. It is particularly useful for planning reports which need to appeal to a wide readership or for emails to be sent to a mailing list, i.e. multiple recipients. Having put the relevant information into the four-box plan, you will be ready to start drafting. First, let's look at this planning tool in more detail.

1 Purpose

Generally speaking, readers decide very quickly whether a document, such as a report or a multiple-recipient email, is relevant to them. Therefore, it is important to:

- capture their interest
- specify the purpose of the document
- inform them what you want them to do, know, or feel.

The '15-second rule' refers to the fact that your readers will take just 15 seconds to decide:

1 what your document is about
2 whether it applies to them.

2 Background or explanation

This section sets the scene for the detail which follows in box 3. To make an impact, your readers may need some additional information to support your key message in box 1. Make sure that you:

- give only the necessary background information. Avoid repeating information they already know
- highlight and extend your key message from box 1 so that it has more impact
- give the information that your readers need in order to agree to your request, solve a problem, analyse a situation, make a decision, etc.

3 Details

This part of your document should include useful and necessary details to reinforce box 2, e.g. schedule, steps in a procedure, technical description, financial information.

Keep this section as short as possible so that readers can follow the development of ideas. Where possible, put supporting information into an appendix. Also remember **not** to include details just to impress your readers.

4 What next?

Repeat the purpose of your document. Make sure your readers clearly know the next steps in terms of:

- who
- what
- when.

Ensure that there are clear channels for future communication, e.g. if more information is required.

1 **Here are the details of a four-box document plan to recommend a new selection process for a company's suppliers. Draw yourself a four-box document plan and put the details into the most suitable box.**

- Categories for supplier evaluation
- Changes to documentation
- Concern about selection of most suitable suppliers – price and quality
- Decision on implementation within 4 weeks
- Directors to review new system
- Discussion at next meeting
- New system
  - Use e-procurement
  - List main advantages
- Old system
  - Based on local suppliers
  - List main disadvantages

- Procedure for introduction
- Proposed timescale for implementation
- Recommend introduction of new evaluation system for suppliers
- Replace existing system with more transparent system
- Results: more transparency and savings
- Training in use of new system

2 **Now decide which element in box 3 could be moved to an appendix.**

3 **Below is a short report on working from home. Read through the report and then map the information into a four-box plan.**

Introduction

In our original report, we proposed to offer the possibility of home-working to a group of employees so that they could carry out the majority of their work at home. This was implemented in April 2011 after the relevant IT and telecommunication links were set up to the office, colleagues, and customers. It is now proposed to extend the possibility of full time home-working to staff who already work from home 20% (one day a week) of the time.

Benefits of home-working

These are:

- improvement to the services provided to customers
- savings in accommodation in terms of both space and cost
- positive implications for both recruitment and retention of staff
- belief that home-working will offer staff the opportunity to balance work with other aspects of their life, in particular care responsibilities
- the opportunity for individuals who previously would have been unable to enter or remain in work to do so
- perception that fewer office interruptions associated with office-based work would result in increased productivity levels.

Challenges of home-working

Home-working employees must agree to:

- stay focused on the job and avoid distractions
- stick to designated hours – clearly schedule the days and hours of work
- set up a work phone number and email address; only give these details out to clients and potential customers
- turn off personal mobile phone and let the home phone go to the answering machine
- plan work and social life separately

Conclusions and next steps

Effectively managed, home-working will continue to increase efficiency and provide cost savings at the same time as maintaining and, in some cases, improving performance. A copy of the 'Cost benefit analysis report' is attached.

Further detailed discussions will be required in order to assess the potential impact of home-working on this new group of employees. Before these discussions, we will hold a general consultation meeting with all department heads on 4 September 2011 to deal with questions and issues. In advance of this meeting, department heads should familiarise themselves with the attached documentation.

Cultural note

Box 1 of a four-box document plan needs to capture the readers' interest. One way of doing this is to inform your readers what you want them to *do, know, or feel*. However, it is important to recognise that not all cultures have the same attitude towards the expression of feelings.

Some cultures, called **affective**, have a tendency to display their emotions more openly and immediately; whilst other cultures, called **neutral**, have a tendency to keep their emotions hidden or controlled. However, neutral cultures are not necessarily cold or unfeeling, and affective cultures are not necessarily impetuous. It is simply the case that the amount of emotion we show is often the result of shared behaviour (cultural norms).

So, when it comes to writing, it is important to bear this contrast in mind. The affective writer may be seen as getting too close to his/her readers; or perhaps overreacting to the situation. On the other hand, the neutral writer may be seen as too remote from his or her audience; or disinterested in the issue.

4 Layout for an email or letter

There are no rules in writing. There are useful principles. – Will Shetterly (American novelist)

The above quote is particularly appropriate when talking about emails. The reason is that this modern channel of written communication does not always have fixed outlines, and different writers adopt different approaches and layouts. As business letters traditionally have a fixed layout, many email writers use this as a starting point for their structure. However, it is important to differentiate between different types of business emails, as follows:

1 formal emails written in the style of business letters
2 emails written in the style of informal letters
3 email exchanges in the style of phone calls, but written down
4 email responses or acknowledgements written in a very concise or informal way, often using no more than a single phrase and an initial as a signature, e.g.

```
Thanks for the info.
John
```

Types 1 and 2 above can generally follow the classical structure of a letter. Here is the typical structure for a business letter:

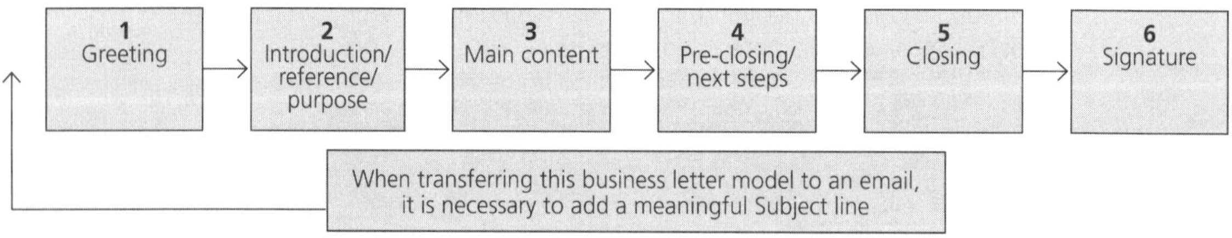

You can find examples of specific language for each of these phases in Appendix 1.

In contrast, types 3 and 4 above generally don't have a formalised structure, as John's brief acknowledgement (above) shows. They have informational content (i.e. they convey a message) but it is difficult to establish any rules for their structure.

So, where does this leave email writers? You need to decide what type of email you are writing. In particular, the formality (or informality) of the relationship with your reader will help you decide whether you need to follow the classical model of a business letter or whether it is appropriate to use a more informal approach. In conclusion, the format of email writing is less about formal rules and more about a flexible approach to email structure: different layouts for different audiences.

Useful tips

For writing formal documents

- Break up your document into meaningful sections so that your reader can easily get an overview.
- Put white space between the paragraphs.
- Don't create unnecessary white space – it makes the document unfocussed and difficult to read.
- Use headings, (bulleted) lists, and bold type to help readability.
- Avoid underlining.
- Use phrases from Appendix 1 to create transparent structure.

For writing informal documents

- Emails can be written as you would speak.
- Remember to remain friendly and polite.

1 **The paragraphs and bulleted lists in the following three emails have been mixed up. Decide in which order the paragraphs should appear and then rewrite the emails in the correct order.**

To: nick.jones@veeyo.com

Subject: Schedule

Lisa

Please could you let me know whether you would be interested in working on the main tasks, as outlined above? For the additional notes, I realise you don't have much information yet and may not be able to give us an answer.

Many thanks for getting back to me so promptly. It's great to hear that you are interested in working with us. Apologies for my delay in replying. I was unwell last week.

We are still looking into your suggestion about the scope of the additional notes. At this stage, we have not made a final decision. I plan to discuss this with my team next week and aim to send you more details over the next two weeks.

With best wishes

With regards to timings and details, we plan to have the main tasks for this project ready by the middle of October. We would send you the task list then, and would like you to devise a number of categories with which to label certain key business categories. We would like to receive the list, arranged according to category, by the middle of November. Please could you let me know whether this would be acceptable to you?

I look forward to hearing from you.

Dear Nick

2

To: Maximore Customers
Subject: Customer Survey

Make your voice heard in just a few minutes

Annetta Sherbourne

With a few simple questions and a few minutes of your time, we can begin to understand what matters to you. We want to increase awareness in the media of the challenges savers face. By sharing your feedback with selected financial journalists we hope to draw attention to the issues that really matter to you and maybe even start the wheels of change. We will of course also use your feedback to see how we can also help you to overcome some of the issues you currently experience as a saver.

Dear Mr Bennett

Win £50 Harwells vouchers

Customer Relations Manager

There can be no denying that we are experiencing times of unprecedented economic uncertainty. As a new UK bank, Maximore believe it's vital that we really understand the issues that savers are confronted with today. Which is why I'm writing to invite you, as a valued Maximore Savings customer, to take part in our first Customer Survey.

As a thank you, on completing the survey you can enter our free prize draw to win one of twenty £50 Harwells gift vouchers.

Kind regards

You will also have the opportunity to join our new Customer Survey Panel. Joining our Panel means you will exclusively be invited to take part in future surveys and have your say on other issues which affect you. And of course, you'll have the chance to win even more vouchers.

Thank you in advance for your time and feedback.

Completing the survey is simple and your answers are anonymous. Just click on the link and follow the instructions online. The survey is open until midnight Sunday 24 October 2011.

Your opinion is important – join Maximore Customer Survey Panel

3

To: stephen@stephenhenley.com
Subject: Expenses Claim

Rotarongan International Airlines Ltd.

- IBAN number:

Having assessed your claim, and as a gesture of goodwill we will credit an amount of GBP100 to your bank account. In order to make the transfer, could you please provide us with the following information:

- costs directly linked to travel delays

Feedback Management

- approved receipts provided

Thank you for your recent claim for reimbursement of expenses, incurred as a result of the disruption to your flight from Rotaronga to London Heathrow. We wish to assure you that we did everything in our power to minimise the consequences for all passengers. Therefore we deeply regret that we were unable to assist you as much as we would have wished in this difficult situation. We apologise for any inconvenience you experienced as a result.

- reasonable expenses incurred

We appreciate you taking the time to inform us about your experience and we hope that this incident will not discourage you and your family from choosing Rotarongan International Airlines in your future travel arrangements.

- Swift code:

Yours sincerely

- Account name:

Dear Mr Henley

As the flight irregularities that occurred were clearly due to 'force majeure', we are only able to offer you limited financial compensation, based on:

Maryam Mobara

- Bank name:

Cultural note

In recent years, email has developed as the channel of choice for both national and international written communication. However, without agreed standards for email writing, writers have felt free to use their own preferred practices, based on cultural norms or personal style.

At an intercultural level, this has led to an emergence of a variety of features, some of which may seem unusual to some writers. One example is the blending of **social** and **professional** exchanges within the same document. Does the writer who starts their email with the phrase 'How are you?' really expect a response? Or is it simply a polite phrase, as one would expect in a face-to-face encounter?

When it comes to emails, a chatty style at the beginning of a professional document might well be a feature of the writer's personality.

5 Linking 1: Connecting sentences

Writing is the best way to talk without being interrupted. – Jules Renard (French author)

Writing needs to flow – from the first line to the last. Just as we talk about a fluent speaker, whose language flows naturally, we can talk about a fluent writer. The techniques for fluent speech and fluent writing are different, but the effect is the same. In fluent writing, the reader can easily follow the internal structure of a document and the connections between the writer's ideas. So, while Unit 4 focused on the external structure of a document in terms of its clear format and layout, this unit will look at techniques for creating a transparent internal structure.

We will look at two types of linking:

1 Logical connections, e.g. *as a result, in contrast, in addition*

2 Chronological connections, e.g. *first, second, after that, finally*

Both types of linking make it easier for the reader to follow the flow of ideas or information. Leaving them out gives the reader a sense of uncertainty and makes it more difficult to read comfortably.

Let's look first at **logical connections**. In the sample text below, the logical linking words are shown in bold:

> *We launched the new products at a time when competition was fierce. **Therefore** it was difficult for us to get the commitment of all our senior management. **In addition**, the high bank interest rates made it hard for us to get the necessary financial backing; **however**, after lengthy negotiations we managed to ...*

Notice how the linking words are used either between sentences (separated by a full stop) or between clauses (separated by a semi-colon).

The linking words and phrases above have very specific meanings:

- *therefore*: cause in the previous sentence; result in the present sentence
- *in addition*: extra information in the present sentence to be read together with the first information given in the previous sentences
- *however*: contrast between expected outcome, based on expectation from previous clause, and actual outcome as stated in the present clause.

You can find a fuller list of logical linking words and phrases in Appendix 2.

Chronological connections, as you would expect, have to do with time and order of occurrence. You can see some uses of chronological linking words in the following sample text. The linking words are shown in bold:

> *I would like to go over the action plan before our next meeting so that we are aligned on the next steps.* ***First of all****, you will need to extract the sales figures from the P&L account.* ***Next****, these figures will require some analysis so that we can see where the major sales outlets are.* ***At the same time****, we will be in a better position to identify where we have incurred significant costs.* ***Finally****, I would like you to put these figures into a spreadsheet and circulate it to the whole team.*

Here the writer shows the time link between ideas or actions, i.e. what comes first, second, next, etc. Chronological links include phrases such as:

- *First/first of all/initially/to start with/the first step/at the first stage*
- *Second/secondly/the second step/at the second stage*
- *Then/after that/next/subsequently/the next step/at the next stage*
- *Finally/the final step/at the final stage*

You can find a fuller list of chronological linking words and phrases in Appendix 2.

Again, the use of these phrases makes the relationship between information and actions explicit and transparent, and, as a result, improves the readability of the text.

Useful tips

- Linking words and phrases show the relationships between your ideas and information.
- They make your writing more fluent and your documents easier to read.
- **Logical** links help the reader to follow the logical relationships between your ideas and information.
- **Chronological** links help the reader to follow the time relationships between information and actions.

1 **Underline the linking words and phrases in the following conclusion from a marketing report.**

> In short, last year was a fantastic year for us. Obviously, we are confident about next year; however, we recognise the risks of over-rapid growth. Therefore, we are going to put in a prudent forecast. For instance, we feel that some of the Far Eastern markets have bounced back too quickly. In addition, Eastern Europe is still somewhat unstable, though it has become a lot firmer in the last few months. In other words, let us not become overconfident. Usually a company in our position would take a very optimistic view of future prospects. Our competitors have. For example, Intersearch is investing huge sums in development. Similarly, QWX has bought a number of smaller providers in various countries. We, too, have been active. In particular, our acquisitions in Northern Europe have taken us into the heart of technological developments. Yet, let us not be complacent. In conclusion, this is a tough market but we can feel quietly confident.

2 **Underline the linking words and phrases in the following extract from a report about Corporate Responsibility.**

In recent years Corporate Responsibility (CR) has moved further and further up the agenda of the world's biggest organisations, but what does CR really mean? In short, CR is the idea that an organisation should choose to demonstrate respect for the rights of workers, local communities, and the environment throughout their operations. In other words, the obligations of the organisation extend beyond what they are legally required to do. In fact, CR encourages organisations to voluntarily try to improve performance in a wide range of areas.

Globalisation has clearly increased the power and impact of transnational organisations but this impact can be both positive and negative. For example, the current media focus on green issues has highlighted public concerns about protecting the environment. Companies, therefore, need to take responsibility and respond to these worries.

CR can bring many benefits to an organisation. For instance, it can help a company establish a clear position in a busy market; alternatively, it can help to protect a particular brand. The process of creating a new set of values and responsibilities can also create a more developed identity for an organisation. However, it is critical for the CR process to be part of the day-to-day running of the company rather than it just being a process to please stakeholders.

3 **The linking words and phrases in the following marketing email have been omitted. Complete the email with a suitable word or phrase from the list below. Note: sometimes, more than one option is possible.**

alternatively	consequently	however	normally
as a result	finally	in addition	of course
but	first of all	in summary	secondly
clearly	for example	naturally	therefore

To: peter.burrows@ecs.co.uk

Subject: New product

Dear Peter

We would like to draw your attention to a new product that we have added to our range. **1** .... , as a stockist of our products, you are aware that customers have been asking for an enhancement to the 'utility' feature on the Alpha model. We have, **2** .... , developed the new Alpha Plus to provide customers with just this function. **3** .... , the new model offers increased efficiency; **4** ...., as you will see, the operation has been simplified by the new 'Quick Start' button. **5** .... , we expect that customers will appreciate the new control panel, which looks much more attractive than in previous models. **6** .... , this is a major renovation for a well-established product, which we believe will be very attractive to your customers.

7 .... , you would expect that the above enhancements would involve an increase in price **8** .... we have managed to negotiate favourable terms with our sub-contractors. **9** .... , we are able to offer you the Alpha Plus at the same price as the Alpha. This compares very favourably with competitor products. The Blaster, **10** .... , retails at £59.99.

11 .... , I hope that this pricing will be an incentive for you to place an initial order for this product.

We are planning a promotional campaign next month, and will be demonstrating the product to our key customers. **12** .... , we would like you to be the first in your region to stock the product. **13** .... , we hope you will take advantage of our free demonstration service. We will be in your area from 13–15 November and our sales rep will be pleased to visit you at a convenient time. **14** .... , if these dates are not suitable, we can arrange a visit at another time.

15 .... , one of our sales team will call you in the next few days to get your feedback. **16** .... , if you'd like to speak to me personally, please call me on 0845 5632 5683.

Regards

Ranjit Mahotra

Regional Sales Director

Cultural note

The texts presented in this unit follow a particular development, going from the general, i.e. presentation of the topic, to the specific, i.e. detailed information. This approach is typical of **deductive logic**. The aim of this pattern is to establish the topic immediately so that people know from the start what you are talking about. After that the details can be presented deductively as they are needed. This is a common Western approach to business communication.

In **inductive logic**, you go from specific to general. The minor points of an argument are stated first and the main point is then arrived at as a conclusion. The focus here is on how the details relate to the whole. Inductive logic requires you to gather the information so that you can reach a logical conclusion. This creates a different feel to communication, making it less rigid than the deductive approach. The inductive pattern is a common Eastern approach to business communication.

6 Linking 2: Sentence structure

All the words I use in my stories can be found in the dictionary – it's just a matter of arranging them into the right sentences.
– W. Somerset Maugham (English playwright and novelist)

In Unit 5, we looked at one aspect of document structure – connectors **between sentences**. In this unit, we will look at another dimension of structure which can further improve the readability of your document. This is the relationship between information **within a sentence**. To do this, we need to differentiate between the following three types of sentence structure:

1 Simple sentences
2 Compound sentences
3 Complex sentences

The following sample sentences from reports illustrate these three types:

1 *The product was launched ten years ago.*

This is a simple sentence consisting of one clause.

2 *Intersearch is investing huge sums in development* ***and*** *QWX has bought a number of smaller providers in various countries.*

This is a compound sentence consisting of two clauses, linked by 'and'. Clauses in compound sentences can also be linked by 'or' and 'but'.

3 *Intersearch,* ***who*** *entered the market recently, is investing huge sums in development.*

This is a complex sentence consisting of two clauses, linked by the relative pronoun 'who'.

Bank interest rates made it hard for us to get the necessary financial backing, especially ***since*** *they were very high initially.*

This is a complex sentence consisting of two clauses, linked by the subordinating conjunction 'since'. Complex sentences consist of two (or more) clauses, linked by either a relative pronoun or a subordinating conjunction.

The main relative pronouns are:

who	which	what	when	where	why	how	that

The main subordinating conjunctions (with the meanings they express) are:

because/ as	if	when/as	after/ before	while	while	so	(al)though
reason	*condition*	*time*	*time*	*time/ contrast*	*purpose*	*result*	*contrast*

We can now compare the various methods of connecting information and ideas within a single sentence. As these sentences demonstrate, the effect is quite different:

*They only set up the operation three months ago **but** they've already gone bankrupt.*

This is vaguer and less emphatic.

***Although** they only set up the operation three months ago, they've already gone bankrupt.*

Here, the subordinate clause is reduced to a less important role.

*They only set up the operation three months ago; **however**, they've already gone bankrupt.*

In this example, more emphasis is placed on 'they've already gone bankrupt'.

None of these techniques is better or worse than the others. However, you need to be aware of these techniques and make your choice on which to use in order to create:

- different effects in your writing
- variety in your writing

Useful tips

- Use a range of techniques to show the relationship between information within a sentence.
- Use linking words and phrases to show the relationship between sentences (see Unit 5).
- Use a variety of sentence structures to make your writing more interesting and engaging.

1 **What type of sentence is each of these? Write the sentence number into the correct column.**

Simple	Compound	Complex
1		

1 The economic crisis has clearly had a significant effect on our business environment.
2 Although our sector has been affected by the impact of the global recession, it has shown a greater resilience than other parts of the economy.
3 As we are all aware, during periods of rapid economic decline, our customers look carefully at their expenditure.
4 We have therefore responded to this pressure on household and business expenses with new price plans that are specifically designed to address customers' needs.
5 If we look at society, our services have clearly become increasingly important in the day-to-day lives of our customers.
6 We see this especially in the way in which our services offer people new flexibility in their business and personal lives.
7 This new flexibility will encourage more growth and lead to more social changes.
8 We have also continued to see pricing pressure in Europe.
9 Because the period of rapid growth in new customer numbers is now over we need to adjust our resources accordingly.
10 So that we can remain competitive, we are committed to reducing operating costs.
11 We will maintain this focus over the coming year and drive down costs.
12 Unfortunately, this involves reducing our workforce but our company will certainly continue to be a good place to work.

2 **In the following text, underline all the words and phrases used to link clauses together within a single sentence. Remember that a subordinate clause may appear at the beginning of a sentence.**

As we are changing the current reporting process, we must keep a clear record of the number of products which we have renewed. This will enable us to monitor our progress more closely. So, when the new version of the XYZ Technical Production Management software is installed, we will be able to maintain this information directly within the database. After all technical reports have been created within the database, we will be able to analyse data directly, which will eliminate the need to request this information from Application Groups via surveys, as it is done today.

The new technical solution will provide us with global visibility on products so that we can see the specific renovations that we have planned. The quality of the database is, of course, dependent upon the quality of the data which has been entered by the Application Groups. Data must be reliable and credible so that it can support analyses within the organisation. It must also allow communication to external partners, when this is relevant. It is, therefore, critical that Application Groups enter and maintain correct data.

3 **The following extract from a report includes simple, compound, and complex clauses. Where there is a gap, complete the sentence with a suitable word or phrase. In some cases, there is more than one possible option.**

Over the last year, our strategy has focused on the development of our new technology for agricultural uses **1** .... we have made significant advances in the commercialisation of the associated products. There was a significant milestone in spring 2010 **2** .... we got approval for the launch of these products. **3** .... we were required to carry out one further study, this did not delay the product launch. This additional work has now been completed **4** .... we hope to have the final results around the end of this year.

During 2009, negotiations were opened with a number of different local companies **5** .... are interested in representing us in Europe. This will help to make us better known in countries **6** .... we currently don't have an office or a representative.

We have also made significant changes to our personnel **7** .... the company has developed into new areas, especially developing contracts and links with industry. Peter Bartlett has been appointed to the post of Managing Director **8** .... I hope you will join with me in congratulating him on this well-earned promotion. Meanwhile, Jane Davies has moved on **9** .... I would like to express our thanks to her for all her work during the early stages of the company. **10** .... we are moving on to this new stage, it is appropriate for Peter to assume that role.

11 .... I look ahead, there are two things which I would like to comment on. We now feel **12** .... the company can move to the stock market in the next two years **13** .... we will investigate that objective at the beginning of next year **14** .... we can be sure to have sufficient capability for the new opportunities **15** .... I described earlier.

So, we are now in a much better position to move forward **16** .... the options have become much clearer. In a year's time, I hope **17** .... we will be able to report on a significant number of events **18** .... have occurred in that period.

Cultural note

The contrast between **structured** and **flexible** styles is commonly used to describe differences in personality. However, it is also a feature of cultures, where some prefer a more planned approach to working, while others prefer a more organic style.

When we look at documents, we can see this difference reflected in approaches to writing. In some cultures, it is important to have a document structure with a clear, logical development of information. In others, more attention is paid to building the relationship with the readers or to creating impact by the flow of ideas. When writing for an international audience, it is important to reflect on one's own preferred writing approach; and also to analyse the approach of others.

7 Recognising and using tone

Tone can be as important as text. – Edward Koch (American lawyer and politician, Mayor of New York City from 1978 to 1989)

Tone in writing refers to the writer's attitude towards:

- the reader
- the subject of the message.

For example, the writer might want to establish a close, friendly relationship with the reader; alternatively she or he might want to communicate in a neutral, formal tone. Or in a request, the writer might think it appropriate to use direct, forceful language; alternatively she or he might want to express the request in a more indirect, collaborative tone. These features fall into the category of tone.

Tone is important and is present in all communication. It affects the relationship and the message as much in writing as it does in speech. Business writers should therefore consider the tone of their message, whether they are writing an email, letter, report, or any other type of business document.

Tone comes from:

- your choice of words
- your sentence structure and sentence length
- the structure, order, clarity, and precision of the information you present.

There are two main challenges for business writers:

1 recognising the range of tones in written documents
2 producing the appropriate tone in your documents

This unit will focus on point 1. Point 2 will be dealt with in Units 8 and 9.

Useful tips

- Tone is about language being appropriate, to your reader and your message.
- Tone is not about right and wrong language; it is about choosing the most appropriate way of expressing yourself.
- Tone comes from your words, your sentences, and your information.
- Tone is important for creating the right relationship with your reader(s).

The following list is a starting point for exploring and recognising the range of tones in communication. Each pair in the list represents a contrast in tone, which can be expressed with language in terms of:

a choice of words

b sentence structure and length

c content

1 **Formal** *'Dear Mr Brown'*	*or*	**Informal** *'Hi Peter'*
2 **Distanced** *'It has come to our attention ...'*	*or*	**Personal** *We have seen ...'*
3 **Precise** *'We expect 236 delegates at our conference.'*	*or*	**Vague** *'There'll be around 250 of us at the meeting.'*
4 **Complex** *'Although procedures vary widely, they share some characteristics, especially in terms of planning and reporting, which are carried out on a monthly basis using the standard software tool that was introduced at the end of last year on the main company sites, except in South America, where it is planned to phase in the tool later this year.'*	*or*	**Simple/straightforward** *'Procedures vary widely, but they do share some characteristics. In particular, planning and reporting are carried out monthly using the standard software tool. This tool was introduced at the end of last year on the main company sites. It will be phased in to South America later this year.'*
5 **Direct** *'Please send the information by 13 January.'*	*or*	**Indirect** *'We would be very grateful if you could send the information by 13 January.'*
6 **Emotional** *'We were totally overwhelmed by the response to our questionnaire.'*	*or*	**Neutral** *'The questionnaire was completed by a large number of people.'*
7 **Assertive** *'The report must be completed by the end of the week.'*	*or*	**Encouraging** *'We hope that you'll be able to complete the report by the end of the week.'*
8 **Task-oriented** *'The minutes of the staff committee meetings should be circulated no later than 48 hours after the meeting.'*	*or*	**Relationship-oriented** *'The minutes of the staff committee meetings are vital for follow-up after our meetings. We therefore expect the minute-taker to circulate the minutes no later than 48 hours after the meeting. If this is not feasible, please contact the chairperson in order to agree a new date for circulation.'*

The email on the next page is fairly **formal**. The writer remains **distanced** from his/her readers, particularly because the email is not directed at one specific recipient. It is fairly **precise** in its content, and the information is somewhat **complex**. It is neither particularly direct nor particularly indirect, but it is definitely **neutral** rather than emotional. Its matter-of-fact presentation of information means that it doesn't really fit into the assertive or encouraging brackets. However, the facts also mean that this text can be categorised as **task-oriented**.

From: customersupport@el-soft.org
Subject: EL-Soft planned service outage
This message is to notify you that EL-Soft is planning a scheduled service interruption on Sunday, 31 October. On this day EL-Soft will move its entire computer centre to a new location and all machines and all services will necessarily be interrupted for a time. The service outage is planned to start at 9.00 a.m. (Eastern Standard Time) and will last for six hours. During this time, no network-reliant services will be available. Affected services will include email, FTP, sales statistics, and website access. However, all mail in transit will be preserved and will be processed normally when service is restored. List Owners may wish to inform their list subscribers of this interruption. We apologise for the inconvenience and we appreciate your selecting EL-Soft for your list-hosting needs. The new computer centre will enable us to serve you better. If you have any questions or concerns about how our move will affect your service, please write to: customersupport@el-soft.org

1 **Look at the following email and decide which tones from the list on the previous page the writer has used. Not all the features from the list apply.**

To: nick@helpathand.com
Subject: Work
Hi Nick Great to hear from you. Many thanks for getting back to me so promptly. Very glad that you're interested in working with us. Apologies for my delay in replying. I was unwell last week. Now on to timings and details. We plan to have the main tasks for this project ready by around the middle of October. Not exactly sure of the date yet, but when the guys have written the project specs, we'll send you all the tasks, and we'd like you to break them down into a number of categories. Your first job will be to put the tasks into the appropriate business category. We'd like to receive your list, arranged according to category, by the middle of November. OK? Please could you let me know whether you'd be interested in working on the main tasks, as outlined above? We really hope you'll agree. For the additional notes, sorry that you don't have much information yet and may not be able to give us an answer. Of course, I understand. I look forward to hearing from you. With best wishes Lisa

2 **The following letter has a very different tone. Decide which tones from the list the writer has used. Again, not all the features from the list apply.**

Investor**Choice**

Hi Kamal

We have some great news for you in these cash-strapped times. Transfer your investment accounts to enjoy our low trading costs – and get up to **£100 cash back**.

InvestorChoice is pleased to announce we will not be increasing our low fees from January. That's right. We won't be charging you a penny more for phone trading. And we won't be passing on any new charges to you in order to cover our own costs. Our low-priced trading charges will remain low. Transfer to us and you'll also receive up to £100 cash back for every account you transfer *(based on 0.5% of the value of the transfer).*

Find out more by talking to one of our agents. Call us now on **0801 987654.**

We look forward to hearing from you.

The team at InvestorChoice

3 **The following document is the end of a report on the potential of online learning. As you read the report, decide which tones the writer has used. Not all the features from the list will apply.**

The potential of online learning

Conclusion

The study shows that, in general, online learning provides clear benefits in terms of:

- scheduling
- flexibility
- costs

However, it is not yet clear whether our current resources (trainers, materials, and approaches) can be adapted to online teaching or whether they will need a total overhaul before we can move forward to creating a new framework for teaching and learning. It is therefore proposed that this report be used as the basis for a future project, which will lay the groundwork for the next steps.

Therefore the following steps will need to be carried out by the end of October:

1. A detailed review of all training materials
2. An assessment of current training approaches
3. A programme of retraining for current trainers

Team members for this study will be appointed within the next two weeks.

Cultural note

The distinction between **direct** and **indirect** tone in communication is both a personal and a cultural feature. Groups that prefer direct communication focus on the explicit meaning of words. They prefer to say what they mean and to deal with conflict directly.

Indirect communicators, however, do not believe that everything needs to be said. They tend to belong to cultures that are more group-focused, rather than individual-focused, so their communication style aims to maintain harmony within the group. They prefer to rely on implied meaning. They avoid conflict and avoid saying 'no'.

8 Varying tone with words and expressions

It is the tone that makes the music. French proverb

A skilled writer can express the same information using a variety of tones. For example, the following phrases all express a request, though with different levels of directness:

Could you please ...?

I'd like you to ...

I'd be grateful if you would ...

Similarly, the following express suggestions:

Let's ...

How about ...?

I suggest that we/you ...

It is recommended that you ...

The difference is in their level of formality. For a list of tone contrasts, refer back to the list in Unit 7.

When we look beyond the phrase at longer texts, **sentence structure** and **vocabulary** combine to create tone. However, it is important for you to be able to both recognise and use each of these separately. In this unit we will concentrate on varying tone by selecting from a range of words or expressions with the same (or similar) meanings. Unit 9 unit will deal specifically with sentence structure and length.

These example sentences say exactly the same thing, but they change the tone using different levels of vocabulary:

I'm sorry but your payment terms are not OK for us.
(simple vocabulary)

I regret to inform you that your payment terms are not acceptable.
(more professional vocabulary)

You wrote that you'd send the document 'by EOD on Friday'. What does this mean?*
(simple vocabulary)

Could you please clarify the meaning of the phrase 'by EOD on Friday'?*
(more professional vocabulary)

*EOD stands for 'end of day' and refers to the end of the business day in whichever time zone the writer is in. You may also see EOB 'end of business', COP 'close of play' or a number of other variations on this theme. They all mean the same thing.

Useful tips

The writer should focus on getting the tone right at two stages of the writing process:

1 when writing the first draft

2 when reviewing and editing the first draft

In fact, many writers omit the second stage – or if they do review their texts, they look at the content, not the tone. To avoid this mistake, you should include tone review as a specific stage in your writing.

1 **The following expressions indicate similar content with different tones. Match the expressions which communicate the same content.**

a It is of the utmost importance that you …
b I am looking forward to seeing you on 17 October.
c I am very pleased that you are able to …
d Dear Mr Bentley
e I would be grateful if you could clarify …
f The next stage of the process is to …
g I would appreciate if you could …
h Don't hesitate to let me know if I can be of further assistance.
i I am writing in connection with …
j I regret to inform you that …

1 See you next week. ....
2 Hi Peter ....
3 This email is about … ....
4 It is good that you can … ....
5 This is not at all clear. ....
6 You must … ....
7 Unfortunately, ...
8 Next we are going to … ....
9 Let me know if I can help. ....
10 Make sure that you … ....

2 **Now look at the pairs of expressions on the next page and decide which aspect of tone they reflect (See Unit 7 for further explanation of the aspects of tone). For each pair of expressions (one on the left and one on the right), choose the feature of tone that is being contrasted. Use each contrast once. The first one has been done as an example.**

~~Formal vs Informal~~
Distanced vs Personal
Precise vs Vague
Assertive vs Encouraging
Complex vs Simple/straightforward
Direct vs Indirect
Emotional vs Neutral
Task-oriented vs Relationship-oriented

See you next week.	*Informal*
Please …	
It is good that it will be possible for you to …	
Secondly we are going to …	
Call me if you need any help.	
Make sure that you …	
We expect to see around 50 participants at the conference.	
I am writing in connection with the last email that you sent.	

I am looking forward to seeing you on 17 October.	*Formal*
I would appreciate it if you could …	
I am very pleased that you can …	
The next stage of the process is to …	
Don't hesitate to let me know if I can be of further assistance.	
I believe that we should …	
48 people have indicated that they will attend the forum.	
Reference is made to your last email.	

3 **The email below could be described as informal, vague, and direct in tone. Rewrite the same email but this time make it formal, precise, and indirect.**

To: dominic321@ailol.com
Subject: Training session
Hi Dominic Just to let you know that we are planning a training session on virtual project management next week. Am trying to find an OK day for everyone. How is Tuesday at 16.00 CET for you? If that works, it'll give everyone a chance to take part. We'll use a conf call to bring all the project guys together. Let me know if you need any technical support. I hope you can join us. Let me know. Regards Jamie

4 **This next email could be categorised as formal, distanced, complex, and neutral in tone. Rewrite it to make it informal, simple, personal, and emotional.**

To: nickhenry@cttinternet.com
Subject: IT support
Dear Nick I am writing in connection with your email, offering IT support to our organisation. The range of services offered is impressive and does, indeed, match our requirements. However, I regret to inform you that there is no possibility at present to increase our current budget for IT services. Therefore it will not be possible for us to take up your generous introductory offer. Going forward, we will monitor the budgetary situation and if it changes, I will definitely contact your organisation. Finally, I would like to thank you again for contacting us. Regards Pavel Stokowicz

Cultural note

One result of changing the tone is to change the relationship with your reader(s). However, when writing in an international context, how can you decide which is the most appropriate tone to use? For example, is there a risk of creating the wrong impression by being too formal or too informal, too direct or too indirect? And, if there is a risk in using the wrong tone, what should one aim for in order to reduce the risk?

While there is no absolute answer to these questions, the keys are to:

- get to know the cultural background of your reader(s)
- try to adapt your writing so that your writing tone is appropriate.

9 Varying tone using sentence structure and sentence length

There is never any justification for things being complex when they could be simple. – Edward de Bono (Maltese physician, author, and inventor)

In Unit 8, you saw how the choice of words and expressions can vary the tone of your writing and affect the relationship with your reader. In this unit, you will see how the following features also contribute to tone:

- sentence structure
- sentence length

In Unit 6, you were introduced to the three main types of sentence structure: simple, compound and complex. Here is a quick reminder.

A **simple** sentence consists of a single clause with a subject and a verb, e.g.

The goods	*have arrived.*
subject	**verb**

or a single clause with a subject, a verb, and a complement, e.g.

We	*have received*	*your email.*
subject	**verb**	**complement**

Simple sentences are usually easy to understand. However, a document with many simple sentences may not be. The reason is that simple sentences tend to be short. As a result, the reader has to continually stop and start reading. So, the process of reading lacks smoothness. Smoothness is important for fluent reading. This paragraph, written in short sentences, demonstrates the stop/start effect.

And what is the tone created by simple sentences? On the one hand, they tend to create a straightforward tone. However, for some readers this straightforwardness may indicate a lack of language knowledge or technical expertise.

A **compound** sentence consists of two or more simple sentences (clauses) connected with 'and', 'or', or 'but'.

The goods have been despatched	*but*	*they have not arrived yet.*
clause 1	**connector**	**clause 2**

A compound sentence, consisting of two clauses, is usually easy to understand. However, longer compound sentences may not be. In addition, compound sentences tend to create a less precise tone. This is because they present all the information at the same level, i.e. each clause is a main clause. This is in contrast to complex sentences (see below). In addition, they lack the straightforwardness of the short simple sentence, which can be used to create a precise tone in a document. As a result, they should be avoided, where there is a more effective alternative.

A **complex** sentence consists of a main clause and a subordinate clause, e.g.

If you require any further information, *please don't hesitate to contact me.*
subordinate clause **main clause**

A complex sentence will become more difficult to understand with each layer of complexity. For example, a sentence consisting of a number of subordinate clauses requires effort to understand, as in the following example:

Your email, which included your offer for services, did not include the essential information about prices, which we will need in order to make a decision about whether to invite you to provide us with references from other customers who have used your services.

Does this mean that complex sentences are to be avoided? Particularly long, complex sentences are usually not effective because they can be confusing. However, complex sentences can be effective because they can combine a number of ideas within a single structure. This allows the reader to read fluently, following the logical development of ideas.

In terms of tone, complex sentences tend to create a seriousness of tone – a series of long complex sentences can become so heavy that the text is unreadable. However, when used carefully, complex sentences will contribute a tone of professionalism to a document.

The conclusions are that:

- sentence structure contributes to the tone of a document
- you should be aware of the effect that the choice of sentence structure has
- you should use a variety of sentence structures to make for more effective writing and more interesting reading
- when Edward de Bono said 'There is never any justification for things being complex when they could be simple', he was correct – but he was not thinking in terms of sentence types!

Useful tips

- **Simple** sentences convey a light, straightforward, precise tone.
- **Compound** sentences are less precise than simple sentences. They are also less serious than complex sentences.
- **Complex** sentences can contribute to a serious, professional tone.
- Reading can become more difficult if you have too many short simple sentences as well as too many long complex ones.
- Edit your document to check that you have used a mix of sentence structures and sentence lengths.

1 **The following extract contrasts the use of simple and complex sentences. This combination gives the text impact (short simple sentences) as well as seriousness (longer complex sentences). As you read the text, label the sentences with:**

[S] for simple sentences [C] for complex sentences

This has been a strong year of recovery, as we continued to focus on the implementation of the plans outlined last year. ☐ Our performance over the last year has increased confidence among customers, colleagues, and shareholders. ☐ The key to recovery is to increase sales. ☐ We are on track to hit our target of £256.2 million. ☐ As we move forward, we expect to see financial rewards to shareholders arising from improved sales performance and our continued focus on cost reductions. ☐

In March, we completed a major refinancing. ☐ This provided cost-effective long-term finance by recognising the value in our property portfolio. ☐ At the same time we retain ownership of these valuable assets. ☐

At our AGM in July, we will be proposing a new incentive framework with arrangements to be put in place over the next ten years. ☐ This will build on last year's plan, applying to around 1,000 senior managers in order to retain and motivate key talent. ☐

The many activities that have taken place this year give encouraging signs that our recovery plan is well on course. ☐ Once again there has been great change for everyone. ☐ However, there is a real sense now around the business that the company has renewed enthusiasm and ambition. ☐ This view is also being echoed by many stakeholders and I would like to thank them, as I did last year, for their continued support and the part they are playing in our recovery plan. ☐

2 **Look at the following email. It only consists of simple sentences, making it hard to read. Edit it by combining some of the sentences to make it:**

- easier to read
- more serious in tone

To: martin.craven@edc.co.uk

Subject: Meeting of 25 April

Hello Martin

Thank you for your email. I am writing to confirm the details of our meeting. The meeting will take place on 25 April. The start time will be 14.00. The meeting will last about 2 hours. We will meet in Room 405.

At the meeting, John and Sarah will present the current status of the project. We would like you to prepare a short presentation for the meeting. Please inform us about the project resources for the future. The meeting room is equipped with a laptop and LCD projector. Bring your presentation on a memory stick. Do you need any further support? Let me know.

In other news, a new member is joining the project team. She will be at our meeting next week. Her name is Louise Devallois. She joined the company 6 months ago. Her background is in packaging. She has considerable international experience. This will be very important for us in the future.

I look forward to seeing you on 25 April.

Regards, Bernard de Haas

3 **Look at the following extract from a report about health and safety. It consists of a series of long complex sentences, making it hard to read. Edit it by dividing some of the sentences into simple sentences to make it:**

- easier to read
- lighter in tone

Make any other changes that you think will improve it. You might find that adding bullet points and numbered lists will help to simplify things.

Health and Safety at Work

It is the policy of our company to take all reasonable steps to ensure the health and safety at work of all employees and to take all necessary steps to implement such a policy by providing a safe working environment and monitoring safe working practices for all employees, especially those whose activities are carried out in the production area where there is a greater risk of injury as a result of the industrial processes which are central to our operations.

The attention of all employees is drawn to the safety rules and procedures, which are displayed throughout the production area and in other locations on the company premises, and employees should be aware that disciplinary action, involving warning, suspension, and even dismissal (in serious cases), will be taken against any employee who is found to have violated these rules and procedures either intentionally or negligently.

As part of the continuous focus on health and safety, the company will consult with all employees periodically (and not less than twice per year) to check what additional measures might be taken to increase awareness of health and safety issues, for example through the use of newsletters, bulletins, and posters, and to ensure that all necessary measures are taken to make our health and safety policy effective and to reduce the risk of injury to employees and contractors.

The company will consult with the employee representatives periodically (and not less than four times per year) and will take whatever measures may be necessary to ensure proper training, supervision, and instruction of all employees in matters relating to their health and safety so that all employees have the right both to be informed about existing and new measures as well as to be trained to deal with events which could lead to injury.

Cultural note

In this unit, you have seen how the tone of a document changes with different sentence structure and different sentence length. In particular, complex sentences, used fittingly, can add a serious and professional tone to your writing. But are these features always the sole objective of business communication? Or is there a role for **humour** in business writing? What about the use of emoticons to add lightness to your emails?

Humour is a feature of all cultures; however, not all cultures share the same sense of humour. Therefore, what might be seen as funny in one culture might be a sensitive issue in another. So, at first sight it would seem safer to avoid humour. However, it is undeniable that a little humour with a light touch can help to build a closer relationship with one's business partners. And, as business relationships are developed through effective communication, humour can facilitate the process of relationship-building.

10 Starting off: Greeting, introduction and reference

I always do the first line well, but I have trouble doing the others.
– Molière (French playwright and actor)

If you are one of those writers who feels overwhelmed by a blank piece of paper or an empty computer screen, this unit will help you overcome your block. The key to starting off your document is to have:

- a reason for writing
- a plan for your document
- some key phrases for the beginning

This unit will focus on the key phrases for writing emails.

The main parts at the beginning of an email include:

1 the greeting
2 the introduction
3 the reference
4 the purpose

Sometimes it is also appropriate to write a **social opening** at the beginning of an email, similar to an expression that would be used in a face-to-face meeting. This would probably go after the greeting.

You can find some key phrases for these parts of an email in Appendix 1.

1 The greeting

e.g. *Dear Mr Reynolds*

Your choice of greeting depends largely on:

- your relationship with your reader
- your attitude towards email as a medium of communication

Addressing your reader by his/her surname creates a distance and formality, which is suitable for some relationships. However, in recent years, emails have evolved as an informal channel of communication. One result of this informality has been the growing use of first names. In addition, email is often used as a substitute for phone calls or face-to-face meetings. This has led to the use of greetings typical in such situations, such as 'Hi' or 'Hello'.

2 The introduction

e.g. *I was given your name by ...*

This can be used for the general context or background to the email. It should help the reader to understand immediately why the email has been sent.

3 The reference

e.g. *On the subject of …*

This points to specific information that will be the subject of the email. This may be:

- a new topic raised by the writer
- in response to another email which has already been received by the writer

4 The purpose

e.g. *I am writing to ask …*

This important part makes a clear statement about the writer's objective(s).

Social openings

e.g. *How are you?*

These reflect:

- the informality of the relationship between the writer and the reader
- the nature of the medium somewhere between writing and speech

1 **Divide the phrases below into the correct categories.**

Greeting	Introduction	Reference	Purpose	Social opening
4				

1 I was given your name by Andreas Schmidt, who suggested that …
2 Just a quick email to confirm …
3 We've had a very rainy summer this year.
4 ~~Hello Debbie.~~
5 I am writing to enquire about …
6 When we met last month, you mentioned that you were interested in …
7 I have received your email of 12 September in which you wrote that …
8 How are you?
9 Ladies and gentlemen
10 Thank you for your email of 4 December about …
11 What's the weather like over there?
12 Dear Peter
13 With reference to …
14 I would like to check that …
15 I recently read your article about …

Useful tips

- Choose an appropriate greeting (Dear, Hello, or Hi) and name (surname or first name), based on your relationship with your reader.
- Use a social opening, when it will help to build the relationship with your reader. When in doubt, don't use a social opening.
- Establish the context for writing; introduce the context in which you are writing and establish a clear reference.
- Give the purpose for writing.

2 **To complete the introductions to the following three emails, choose an appropriate phrase from the box below. Use each phrase only once.**

a How are you? It's much too hot for work here.
b Hi Jackie
c I am pleased to learn that the dates for the programme are now confirmed.
d Dear Mr Fields
e I am writing now to ask whether I need to book the travel or whether your office will do it.
f I am writing now to enquire whether you are interested in meeting me when I am in Manchester next month to find out more about our services.
g Hello Andreas
h I was given your name by John Spalding, who mentioned that you might be interested in our services.
i Thanks for your last message about the timetable for the assessment.

1 ....

2 .... SP Components is a supplier of a wide range of parts for the motor industry. We can provide next-day delivery throughout most of the country.

3 ....

4 ....

5 ....

6 .... The schedule is absolutely fine for me.

7 ....

8 ....

9 ....

Once I hear back from you, I will make any further arrangements that may be needed.

3 **Below is a chain of email introductions. Mr Brackley and Ms Shorter are discussing a job opportunity. Complete the gaps with a suitable phrase. Note that there are many possible answers.**

> Dear Ms Shorter
>
> .... in the *Spottisberg Standard* for a laboratory assistant to work in your research department …

> Dear Mr Brackley
>
> .... about the laboratory assistant position to work in our research department. .... you for interview on …

> Dear Ms Shorter
>
> ...., I would like to confirm that the date proposed is fine for me.

> Dear Mr Brackley
>
> .... for interview yesterday. .... that you have not been successful on this occasion. We felt that …

> Dear Ms Shorter
>
> .... that I have not been chosen for the position of research assistant. Thank you for letting me know.

Cultural note

The term **interpersonal space** describes the distance between speakers in a conversation or interaction. On the one hand, there are clearly different distances for different contexts, ranging from intimate situations with family and close friends to public situations when addressing groups of people. On the other hand, intercultural research shows that this behaviour is culturally conditioned. In other words, the physical comfort zone between communicators from different cultures varies.

Although this feature is more observable in face-to-face contact, the same effect may happen in written communication. For example, an informal writing style in either a greeting or a social opening may make the reader feel uncomfortable as the writer has not kept the expected interpersonal distance from the reader. For this reason, it is important in international communication to think carefully about what is acceptable in your culture, as well as what is acceptable in your reader's culture.

11 The main part: Signalling intentions

Words are the most powerful drug used by mankind. – Rudyard Kipling (British writer)

In previous units, you have seen the importance of clarity and transparency for effective writing. This unit will look at one dimension of clear and transparent writing: **signalling intentions**. This phrase means that you explain to your readers the reason(s) for writing. Below are some sample phrases categorised by their intention.

Intention	Sample phrase
Requesting	I would be grateful if you could …
Informing	I am pleased to inform you …
Asking for clarification	Could you supply us with more information …
Making suggestions Drawing attention and reminding	I propose that … I would like to point out …

You can find a full list of phrases for signalling intentions in Appendix 1.

If you are writing a short email, then you will signal your intention in the 'purpose' section (see Unit 10), which gives a clear statement about your objective. However, if you are writing a longer email, then you may have a number of objectives or points, where each one is written in a separate paragraph.

In summary, effective writing means helping the reader:

- understand your intentions in each paragraph of your document, and
- follow the detail in each paragraph of your document.

Appendix 1 will enable you to choose phrases that can be used in a paragraph (usually at the beginning or the end) to clarify your intention.

Units 4 and 14 list techniques to help your reader follow the details.

Useful tips

- Clear and transparent writing makes for easier reading.
- State your overall reason for writing at the beginning of your email.
- Help your reader follow both the structure and objectives within the main part of your email.
- Divide your main part into meaningful paragraphs.
- Use key phrases from Appendix 1 to signal your intentions in each paragraph.

1 **Choose the correct intention for each key phrase.**

a Expressing improbability	**d** Refusing a request	**g** Requesting
b Making suggestions	**e** Asking for approval	**h** Informing
c Acknowledging	**f** Giving bad news	**i** Giving assurance

1 I note that you have … ....
2 We hope that you will have no objection to … ....
3 It is unlikely that … ....
4 I will do my best to ensure that … ....
5 I'm afraid that … ....
6 We would like to tell you that … ....
7 We strongly recommend that … ....
8 Unfortunately, we are unable to … ....
9 I would appreciate it if you could … ....

2 **Here are a further nine key phrases, but they have been mixed up. Reorder the words to create a useful phrase. The intention is provided to help you.**

1 ***Offering:*** would be / I / if you're / interested,/ happy to ....
....

2 ***Providing documentation:*** attached / find / please ....
....

3 ***Asking for clarification:*** explain / could / please / you ....
....

4 ***Expressing urgency or necessity:*** important / it / very / is / that ....
....

5 ***Giving good news:*** you / delighted / that / will / to hear / be ....
....

6 ***Confirming:*** in / I / now / a / am / confirm / position / to ....
....

7 ***Expressing disappointment:*** I / very / unable / you / sorry / am / that / are / to
....

8 ***Reminding or highlighting:*** I'd / like / draw / your attention / to / to ....
....

9 ***Expressing wishes:*** would / to / I / much / like / very ....
....

3 **In the following main part from an email, choose which intention is missing and circle it. Then, write an appropriate phrase into each gap. You can take the key phrases from exercises 1 and 2 above, or you can find alternative phrases in Appendix 1.**

1 ***[Confirming/Giving good news]*** .... the next steps for our collaboration in the FastForward project. Firstly, we will send you a document describing your responsibilities within the project. This document requires careful reading, as it will provide the basis for our relationship. Once you are satisfied with all the terms and conditions, **2** ***[Providing documentation/Requesting]*** .... print and sign two copies of the document and return them both to me.

3 ***[Expressing urgency or necessity/Offering]*** .... this document is returned by 15 December. This date will be the start date of the project and we need to have all parties on board by then. If you are not able to return the document by this date, **4** ***[Giving assurance/Giving bad news]*** .... our offer will be withdrawn with immediate effect.

5 ***[Refusing a request/Requesting]*** .... change any of the dates in the project schedule, as requested in your offer of services. Therefore, please ensure that your sub-suppliers are able to observe the schedule, as you will be responsible for any delays in delivery. **6** ***[Reminding or highlighting/Asking for approval]*** .... the penalty clauses for late delivery. In the past, these terms have caused some confusion. The current terms replace previous terms and shall take effect from the project start date. **7** ***[Asking for clarification/Making suggestions]*** .... you seek legal advice before entering into this contract. Of course, our lawyers will be happy to liaise with your lawyers over any issues requiring further clarification.

8 ***[Providing documentation/Confirming]*** .... the following documents:

1. scope of responsibilities
2. terms and conditions of collaboration (one copy for reference)

Your signature is required on two copies of item 1.

4 **You work in the training department of a large company. You have been asked to write an email to middle management colleagues in the company to find out their professional training needs for the next year. On the next page you will find the beginning and ending of your email. You should complete the main part, using the words in italics as inspiration.**

To: Department heads
Subject: Staff training
Dear colleagues I am writing with regard to further professional development, as discussed in our last meeting. **1** ***[Confirming]*** *budget/agreed*. This will enable us to organise about thirty training days over the next year. **2** ***[Expressing improbability]*** *able/all/without exceeding*. However, depending on the number and range of requests, we may be able to negotiate additional budget at our half-yearly meeting. **3** ***[Expressing urgency or necessity]*** *everyone/responds/email*; otherwise not all needs can be considered and your team members could miss out on opportunities for training. **4** ***[Giving bad news]*** all *training/done/on premises*. I understand that some of you would like to send colleagues to out-of-house courses but, under the current financial circumstances, this is unlikely to be possible. **5** ***[Offering]*** *discuss/individual requests*. Please feel free to contact me by phone or email. The deadline for receiving requests is 12 September. This will give me enough time to analyse your requests and get back to you with training proposals by the middle of October. Regards James McGee Training Manager

Cultural note

One of the features highlighted by acclaimed Dutch social psychologist Geert Hofstede in his research on cultural dimensions for international business is '**uncertainty avoidance**'. This dimension of intercultural difference indicates the extent to which a culture programmes its members to feel either uncomfortable or comfortable in unstructured situations.

In the context of business writing, overall clarity is one way of reducing the risk of misunderstanding. More specifically, the techniques for signalling intentions in written documents, illustrated in this unit, contribute to greater transparency of writing and increase the probability that your objectives and intentions will be understood.

12 Finishing off: Next steps, pre-closing, and farewells

Great is the art of beginning, but greater is the art of ending.
– Henry Wadsworth Longfellow (American poet)

With the end of your document in sight, there is often a temptation to rush the final stage. The key to an effective close to your document is to make sure that your reader knows what is going to happen next. We'll call these the 'next steps'. With this stage completed, you should close the document with suitable phrases for:

- pre-closing
- farewell

This unit will focus on emails and minutes. You can find the key phrases for emails in sections 4–6 of Appendix 1.

1 Next steps

One way of defining the next steps is by using the 3 W's: **what**, **who**, and **when**.

- **What** will define the action to be taken
  e.g. *We will need to analyse the information before we can make a decision.*
- **Who** will define the person with responsibility for the action
  e.g. *Peter has agreed to do this.*
- **When** will define the deadline for completion of the action
  e.g. *The deadline is 24 April.*

Using the 3 W's will help you to check that you have covered the most important elements for the next steps.

Clarifying next steps is important in a range of document types, including emails and minutes. In minutes, where there is usually a time gap between the meeting and the circulation of the minutes, the next steps section is particularly important so that roles, responsibilities, and timeframes or deadlines are clearly defined, as shown in the summary box below.

Agenda Item		**Next Steps**		
Topic	Discussion	Action (WHAT)	Person responsible (WHO)	Timeframe/ Deadline (WHEN)
1.				
2.				
3.				

The following sentence from the minutes of a meeting captures the 3 W's:

Pete (WHO) to analyse the figures (WHAT) by 24 April (WHEN).

2 Pre-closing

In emails, the pre-closing bridges the gap between the main content of the document and the social farewell. While it rarely adds any new business content to the email, it is seen as a polite way of making the transition to the end of the document, e.g.

If you have any further questions, please contact me.

I look forward to meeting you.

When the pre-closing sentence is omitted, the ending of the email may sound too abrupt.

3 Farewell

As noted in Unit 4, in recent years emails have evolved as an informal channel of communication. One result of this informality has been the growing use of informal farewells, such as *Regards* or *Best wishes*. These farewells have the effect of creating a closeness between the writer and the reader that may not be intended for the business relationship. However, more formal farewells, such as *Yours sincerely* and *Yours faithfully*, which were widely used in business letters, are gradually disappearing.

Useful tips

- Use the 3 W's to clarify the next steps.
- Use a polite pre-closing phrase to round off your email.
- Choose an appropriate farewell, based on the relationship with your reader.

1 **In which part of a document do each of these phrases belong? Write the numbers into the table.**

Next steps	Pre-close 1: Offering further assistance	Pre-close 2: Friendly sign-off	Pre-close 3: Final thanks	Farewell
	1			

1 Let me know if you need any more help.
2 I look forward to receiving your report.
3 Thank you for your understanding in this matter.
4 Could you please confirm that you can …
5 Best wishes …
6 I am looking forward to meeting you on …
7 Thanking you in advance.
8 Regards
9 We would like to finish this phase by …
10 Thank you once again for your assistance.
11 The plan for the next phase is:
12 If you have any further questions, please contact me.
13 See you next week
14 Yours sincerely
15 Do not hesitate to contact us again if you require further assistance.

2 **The table below shows the notes from a staff meeting.**

Agenda Item		Next Steps		
Topic	Discussion	Action (WHAT)	Person responsible (WHO)	Timeframe/ Deadline (WHEN)
1. Recruitment	*1. 22 new jobs* *2. recruitment drive now* *3. hard to get people in post – long checks*	*Possible to reduce?*	*DB*	*Info at next meeting*
2. Turnover	*down 3%: uncertain job market*	*Monitor*	*AF*	*Info at next meeting*
3. Sickness	*6%: too high*	*Make questionnaire*	*RP*	*30 September*
4. Staff development	*1. Away Day successful.* *2. Suggestion: plan another for spring*	*1. Contact local training organisations* *2. Get ideas* *3. Circulate info*	*HM*	*1 December*
5. Christmas party	*1. Budget has been slashed* *2. Suggestion: Xmas party held in office to save on venue costs* *3. No agreement*	*1. Contact party planners for quotes* *2. Circulate info*	*AF*	*1. 1 September* *2. Decision next meeting*

The minute-taker is writing up the minutes using the above notes, but has yet to put in the next steps. Choose the right sentences to complete the minutes below.

a A decision to be taken at the next meeting.

b AF to monitor the position and report back at next meeting.

c DB to check if this could be reduced.

d HM to circulate info by 1 December.

e Deadline for questionnaire design: 30 September.

f HM agreed to contact local training organisations to get ideas for themes.

g DB to report back at next meeting.

h AF to contact party planners to investigate financial and practical logistics.

i RP to design a questionnaire to find out more about reasons for absence.

j The results to be circulated by 1 September.

Minutes from Staff Meeting, 11th August

1. Recruitment

It was noted that 22 new positions had been created and a recruitment drive was under way. There was still some difficulty in bringing people into the posts, due to the time taken for pre-employment investigations. ....

....

2. Turnover

Has gone down by 3% – a reflection of the insecurity in employment market. ....

....

3. Sickness

Absence remains at 6%. This is considered too high. ....

....

4. Staff development

IB reported on successful Away Day for senior staff. It was recommended that another Away Day be timetabled for next spring. ....

....

5. Christmas party

It was suggested that significant savings could be made by holding the Christmas party in the office. This would allow more of the reduced budget to be spent on catering and entertainment. The staff at the meeting could not agree. ....

....

....

Cultural note

One of the key aspects of laying out the next steps is to define the timescale or deadline for a task. Although every day consists of 24 hours, not all cultures share the same understanding of how time works.

In **monochronic cultures** people see time as divided into fixed elements – seconds, minutes, hours, days. Tasks can then be organised and scheduled within a specific time block. This sense of time contrasts sharply with that shared by people from **polychronic cultures**. For them time is continuous and not divisible. Where the **monochron** prefers to do one thing at a time, working on a task until it is finished, the **polychron** prefers to work on many tasks at the same time, switching comfortably from one activity to another. For the polychron, this way of working is both stimulating and productive. While monochrons organise their activities around schedules and value promptness, polychrons place emphasis on relationships. The result is that timeliness will depend on the 'importance' of the person in the hierarchy. This contrast has obvious implications in an international context for agreeing the schedule for next steps – and for its fulfilment.

13 Writing clearly and simply

To write simply is as difficult as to be good. – W. Somerset Maugham (English playwright and novelist)

In this unit, we will focus on the process of writing – in particular, writing clearly and simply. In general, clear and simple documents are easier to write and also easier to understand. So, what are the significant factors that contribute to simple writing and easy reading? They are:

1 Knowledge of vocabulary
2 Sentence length and sentence structure
3 Paragraph length
4 Subject knowledge and cultural knowledge
5 Technical knowledge
6 Density of ideas
7 Level of reasoning

Of these seven factors, the first three are the most important for clear and simple writing, so let's look at each of them in a little more detail:

1 Knowledge of vocabulary

Here are three easy guidelines to make sure that you choose the right vocabulary:

1 Use words that you know. Try to avoid using a dictionary to find words, unless you are sure what they mean.

2 Use vocabulary that your reader knows. If you are writing to a professional from the same area as yours, then it is likely that they will share a common vocabulary with you, including technical terms. You can therefore use these terms with a reasonable expectation that your reader will understand them.

3 Most importantly, if you are writing to someone who doesn't share your professional area, then you may need to simplify your vocabulary to make it understandable.

2 Sentence length and sentence structure

Sentence length refers to the number of words in a sentence. The ideal average sentence length for business writing is between 15 and 20 words. However, don't make all your sentences the same length. Vary it to make your writing interesting and engaging. Use short sentences for impact; longer sentences for supporting information.

Sentence structure refers to the type of sentence construction – simple, compound, or complex. (See Unit 6 for a full explanation of these three types). There is also a link between sentence structure and readability. At first sight, simple sentences would seem easier to read. However, a series of them makes your document fragmented and difficult to read. On the other hand, long complex sentences can also make your document hard to follow. The recommendation is, therefore, to vary your sentence structure.

Use bullet points to make lists of items easier for:

- you to write
- the reader to read
- the reader to remember.

3 Paragraph length

Firstly, you should aim to keep your paragraphs between two and six sentences long. Just as with the length of sentences, your reader's attention will drop the longer your paragraphs are. Secondly, start your paragraph with a topic sentence so that your reader knows what the subject of the paragraph is. Thirdly, use a heading, where appropriate, to make the theme of the paragraph clearer.

Useful tips

- Have a mix of shorter and longer sentences.
- Where you have a long sentence with several commas, consider splitting it into several sentences.
- Where you have a series of short sentences, consider combining some of them into a longer sentence.
- Use paragraphs, headings, and (bulleted) lists to help readability.
- Use words that your readers know; don't use long words to impress you readers.

1 **Compare these two extracts from a report on sustainability and list the techniques used in the second version to make it clearer and simpler.**

Version 1

Sustainability means being able to continue indefinitely. This is done by minimising environmental and social impacts. It can also ensure financial stability. Developing your business more sustainably can help you reduce your costs, control risk, improve your reputation, and create new business opportunities. For example, you might reduce wasted energy, water, or raw materials and so make the best of new markets for innovative or better performing products, and, as well as helping the environment and society at large, becoming more sustainable directly benefits the financial performance of your business. But while one-off improvements are worthwhile, you should use a strategic approach to make the most of your opportunities. For example, you might drive long-term change by establishing key objectives and implementing a management system to help you achieve them.

Version 2

Sustainability means being able to continue indefinitely by minimising environmental and social impacts. It can also ensure financial stability. Developing your business more sustainably can help you:

- reduce your costs
- control risk
- improve your reputation
- create new business opportunities.

For example, you might reduce wasted energy, water, or raw materials. This could help you make the best of new markets for innovative or better performing products. As well as helping the environment and society at large, becoming more sustainable directly benefits the financial performance of your business.

However, while one-off improvements are worthwhile, you should use a strategic approach to make the most of your opportunities. For example, you might drive long-term change by establishing key objectives and implementing a management system to help you achieve them.

2 **Adapt the following document to make it simpler and clearer, simply by splitting up some of the longer sentences.**

How to Start an E-Commerce Business

Today, the growth of affordable technology has made business opportunities accessible to almost anyone with a computer and a connection to the Internet. In the past, opening a business was a huge commitment in terms of finances and risk as traditional business owners typically had to give up their jobs, negotiate bank loans, and sign leases before they even generated a single penny of turnover. So, it is not surprising that 95% of them faced bankruptcy within five years. Today, business opportunities are available to anyone with ambition who is willing to put in the time and effort to learn about the world of e-commerce and best of all, you can establish an e-commerce business with minimal funds and very little risk.

The first step to creating your own e-commerce business is to find your niche, for example by examining your hobbies and interests for potential business ideas or by opening a business that is similar to your current job, where you have insider knowledge. Now that you have a few business ideas, it is time to investigate the demand because if you plan to sell to the general public, you'll want to find out how many people are looking for your products or services. Next, find out your would-be competitors, check their websites, and spend some time exploring each one to get an idea of what you are up against.

In order to conduct business, you will need to establish a business entity and go through the various formalities of registration. When you are registered as a legitimate business owner, it is time to open a business bank account. After that, you can start creating your website. One of the keys to successful e-commerce businesses is a professional website as your website is the first and often the only impression your visitors will have of your business.

3 **The following email is unclear because the sentences are too simple and there is a lot of unnecessary information. Rewrite it to make it clearer.**

To: hjohnson@isleton.gov.uk
Subject: Application for post of assistant
Dear Mr Johnson I am writing to apply for the assistant position advertised in the *Evening Post*. As requested, I am enclosing my résumé. Let me introduce myself. My name is Élise Boulanger. I am currently working as an assistant at Burgil's HQ. My email address is eliseboulanger@burgil.com I obtained a commercial diploma in 2000. Then I worked for 4 years as HR administrative assistant for a local food company. During that time I spent 2 months in Barcelona learning Spanish. Upon my return, I joined AFV's HR Department as 'on-the-job training' administrative assistant. My main task was the organisation of specific training for the company's technical personnel worldwide. I also organised language classes for all AFV's employees. Four years later, I joined the Zone Americas HR team. There, I worked on transfers to the markets. I was also responsible for welcoming expatriates to the head office. During the next 7 years, I worked for the Productivity Team. I was the assistant to a team of 60 people. I was also given the opportunity to work for 5 months at AFV's Portugal Head Office. There I worked as an assistant to the Public Relations Manager. During the last few years, I have also developed my organisational skills. I have organised two workshops per year with about 100 participants. Throughout my past jobs, I have developed my international skills. Thanks to the diversity of nationalities, I have also improved my language skills. I am bilingual in French and Italian. I am also fluent in Spanish and Portuguese. I have a good working knowledge of English. Please feel free to contact me if you have any questions regarding my application. I look forward to hearing from you. Élise Boulanger

Cultural note

Clear and simple communication (both in speech and writing) is an agreed target for almost everyone working in an international environment. Global corporations put it into their mission statements and leadership principles; and companies invest in training their staff to be better at communicating around the world. However, what constitutes clear and simple communication differs both between national cultures and between individual personalities. Some cultures tend to value detail and to make decisions based on **precision**; others prefer a general overview and emphasise the **big picture**. Both would claim that they value clarity and simplicity. However, their underlying values make their expectations of clarity and simplicity, well, just different.

14 Writing transparently

Have something to say, and say it as clearly as you can. That is the only secret. – Matthew Arnold (British poet and cultural critic)

Clarity is achieved by using the following techniques:

- setting a clear format for your document (Unit 4)
- using linking words and phrases (Unit 5)
- varying sentence structure (Unit 6)

In this unit we will focus on techniques to make your document more transparent in a visual sense. In general, visually transparent documents are simpler to navigate around (to skim) and therefore easier to understand.

Here are some of the techniques that you can use:

1 headings
2 bulleted and numbered lists
3 page numbering
4 underlining and italics
5 font weights

1 Headings

Use headings to label the major sections and subsections of your document. This is necessary for longer documents. Make sure that each heading is short and meaningful so that your reader can easily scan your document to understand its overall organisation. Finally, don't use too many headings – only about two or three headings per page of text; and don't use capitals *and* bold, or capitals *and* underlining, for headings.

2 Bulleted and numbered lists

Lists help readers to find the most important points within a longer stretch of text. In this way, they help you to present complex information in a more digestible and memorable format. To be memorable, they should be short and to the point. Try to avoid bulleted lists for long sentences.

Modern word processing programs provide many options for bullets, e.g. ■ ◆ ❍ ❐ . These allow the writer considerable creativity in the design of documents. However, it is preferable to use a simple bullet point that is easy to read, i.e. •

Bulleted items do not usually end with a full stop unless they are complete sentences. When writing a bulleted list with phrases, put a full stop after the last item in the list. The sentence introducing your bulleted list should start with a colon (:)

e.g. *The following documents are needed to complete your application:*

Use numbered lists when you are working with instructions to be done in sequence, and the numbers suggest an order. This also applies when you want your reader to refer to specific items by number. If numbers are not essential and the list can be re-ordered without losing its meaning, use bullets.

3 Page numbering

Do not forget to number your pages – either at the top or the bottom.

In reports, the title page is Roman numeral i, but is not shown on the document. The pages that appear before the main content of the report starts are written in Roman numerals ii, iii, iv, etc. The main content of the report starts with page 1.

4 Underlining and italics

Underlining can be used to emphasize words within a text. It can also be used to highlight headings. It is often an alternative to using a bold font, for example in a heading.

Italics can also be used to highlight certain words or to differentiate them from others within the text. In general, italics and underlining do the same job; therefore, it would be unusual to use both within the same text.

In addition to emphasis, italics are used for:

- widely-used loan words from other languages, e.g. The results *per se* (in themselves) are not conclusive; however, they indicate a strong likelihood.
- the first use of foreign words in a text, e.g. The German word *Effizienz* is often translated as 'effectiveness'.
- titles of works, books, reports, etc.

5 Font weights

Another way to attract the attention of your reader is to set some text in **bold**. **Use bold to emphasise important points**; use italics or underlining to *highlight words*. However, be careful not to overuse bold type, as whole paragraphs of text set in bold are hard to read. Bold type creates emphasis because it slows down the reader and forces their eyes to concentrate more carefully on the text. Remember, though, that if you slow them down too much, they may just miss out the text as it takes too long to read.

Useful tips

- Use headings to help your reader see the overall structure of your document. Use these techniques to highlight:
  1. separate sections of your document
  2. key information in your document
  3. specific details in your document
- Don't overuse these techniques, especially bold and underlining.
- Always check that you have used the techniques consistently throughout your document.

1 **In the following text, the headings are missing, and the bullet points and numbering have been removed from lists. Choose the most appropriate heading for each paragraph from the choice below. Then, decide where you would put in bullets and numbering to make the document easier to read.**

Environmental policy	People
Future outlook for the business	Research and development
Main uncertainties	Turnover
Operating costs	

....

Our revenue has continued to grow for the 9th consecutive year. Although sales have only achieved growth of 1%, this is still an excellent achievement considering the world economy during this period.

....

We have focused on our costs this year and have chosen to be quite defensive. Our targets have been to reduce hiring, to re-engineer our products, to refocus our marketing efforts, and to drive our cost base down. The difficult times have made this necessary and our overall performance has been improved by our new finance team.

....

We continue to invest in the quality and design of our products. We believe continued investment in this area is fundamental for two reasons. Firstly, to continue the growth of the business; and secondly to create new products for the future.

....

The company as a whole continues to look for ways to develop our policy. It is our objective to improve our performance by focusing on better waste treatment, more efficient energy use, and improved indoor air quality.

....

Our strategy remains the same: to grow the company internationally. This year has seen the most difficult period for the UK and world economy in living memory. On balance this has done us no harm. This alone makes us very optimistic for the future. Given that we have survived the last twelve months, we should be well placed to for any future recovery.

....

The management of the business and the nature of the company's strategy are subject to a number of risks. The directors have set out the principal risks facing the business. These are the continued economic downturn, the high proportion of fixed costs, our out-of-date products, and the fluctuations in currency exchange rates.

....

We have a very dedicated team that is focused on creating the best possible service we can provide. I would like to thank them all for the hard work and commitment over the past year.

2 **In the text below, the following features have been removed:**

- **underlining**
- **font types (italics and bold)**

Rewrite the document in order to improve its transparency.

New Finance Opportunities

A recent report by the Chicago Institute of Bankers, entitled New Developments in Developing Country Financing has refocused attention on mashwa-hattan, or micro-financing, as it is better known to us. This publication, part of the New Developments in Global Financing series, has become a standard work for economists wishing to find out about key issues around the world. The authors of the current work state emphatically that they do not want to promote mashwa-hattan as the sole way of motivating grass-roots entrepreneurs. However, they do say that mashwa-hattan has created not only an alternative method of financing, but also a new spirit of independence amongst many poorer people, resulting in significant increases in per capita income among the rural population. A recent article in the Times of Rotaronga pointed to real progress in the rural economy since its introduction. In a recent statement, Afran Segozzi, the Minister for Rural Affairs, welcomed these new initiatives, saying that they had made a positive contribution to finifranga, the Rotarongan term for the rural economy.

Cultural note

Is there a right and wrong way to create a business document? The answer to this question will come, at least in part, from your cultural background. Those coming from **universalist** cultures are more comfortable if they are given (or can find) the right way. On the other hand, those from **particularist** cultures are comfortable with fewer rules and therefore greater ambiguity. So, depending on your cultural perspective, you may be looking for the *right way* to create a business document; or you may be happy with a variety of *alternative techniques* that you can draw on.

15 Writing quickly

Don't get it right, just get it written. – James Thurber (American author and regular contributor to *The New Yorker* magazine)

One of the biggest challenges when writing in a foreign language is to write quickly. Of course, it would be unrealistic to expect that you can write as quickly in English as in your first language. However, the amount of time needed should be realistic in relation to the writing task. So, if you feel you are spending too long on writing your emails, minutes, and reports, then you need to reconsider the efficiency of your writing process.

The following flow chart is a starting point for looking at how you approach the writing process. By considering what you could or should be doing at each stage, hopefully you can streamline the process.

1. Think about your reader(s):
   What is ***your*** purpose in writing to them?
   What are ***their*** expectations from your document?

↓

2. Make a start: collect information
   Note down the information to support stage 1.

↓

3. Select the relevant information (focus on content)
   From the information noted down at stage 2, choose only the information that is relevant for your purpose and your reader(s)

↓

4. Write your first draft (focus on structure and style)

↓

5. Once you have your ideas down in your first draft, then you can edit the document in detail.

↓

6. Finally, revise and write a final draft.

In this unit, we will concentrate on successfully completing stage 4 of this flow chart – the first draft. Stages 5 and 6 are part of the 'editing' process and will be covered in Unit 16.

Here are some guidelines to stick to when writing your first draft:

1 Put the selected information from stages 1–3 into a structured framework for your document.
2 Don't focus on language accuracy in your first draft – that comes later. Concentrate on getting your ideas and information down on paper as concisely as possible.
3 Quickly read through your first draft, focusing on:
   - conciseness and relevance of content
   - transparency of structure
   - appropriateness of style
4 Make necessary changes until you are satisfied with the *information* and the *structure.*
5 If time permits, you can now leave a longer document and return to it later for detailed editing. For a shorter document, now move on to detailed editing (see Unit 16).

Useful tips

- Use the procedure in the above flowchart to write your first draft quickly.
- Give yourself a (reasonable) time limit to write the draft, then stick to it.
- Don't be afraid to use lists to capture your information and ideas.
- Do not focus on accuracy – you will edit your document later.

1 **Your company regularly organises an end-of-year party for all the employees and their children. However, this year there has been a suggestion to give the party money to a children's home, where it could be used to buy presents for the children. You work in the Administration Department and have been asked to write an email to all employees to ask them about their preferences. You have completed stages 1–3 from the above flowchart. Now write your first draft (stage 4).**

```
Subject: end-of-year party
Objective: to get feedback from the staff
Background: - annual end-of-year party = party for employees and their children
            - alternative suggestion = to give party money to a children's home

Issues: 1. Party
     - expensive with presents, entertainment, and big lunch for children and parents
     - good opportunity for socialising and building relationships between
       colleagues
     2. Children's home - children have very little and would appreciate presents

Options:  1. continue with party
          2. give money to children's home
          3. ?
```

2 **You are Head of Information Technology in a company with an unwritten policy on work clothes. Male employees should wear ties and jackets; female employees smart dresses, skirts, or trousers. However, some staff working in your IT department have started wearing casual clothes – jeans, T-shirts, trainers, etc. You have decided to write an email to your IT staff. Use the notes below that you have made in stages 2–3 of the writing process to write your first draft (stage 4). You can add any other ideas that you would like to. Try to be firm, but polite.**

```
Subject: work clothes
Objective: to get agreement on dress code from the IT staff
Background: - normal dress code
            - IT current standards of dress

Issues:     - Bad feeling among other staff
            - Image with visiting customers and clients

Options:    1. agree on formal clothes for IT
            2. agree on different dress code for IT
```

3 **You took the following notes at a recent employee committee meeting. Use the notes to finish your first draft of the minutes on the next page.**

Agenda Item		**Next Steps**		
Topic	Discussion	Action (WHAT)	Person responsible (WHO)	Timeframe/ Deadline (WHEN)
1. Communication in meetings (AB)	*Questions:* *1. Are there too many meetings?*	*1. Review the number of meetings*	*1. AB to propose a reduced schedule of meetings for next year*	*by May 2011*
	2. Are meetings efficiently run?	*2. Streamline the procedures for meetings*	*2. JC to organise training in effective meetings*	
2. Foreign travel (JL)	*Requests for:* *1. Special compensation for weekends away*	*1. Review payments*	*1. VD*	*1. By next meeting*
	2. Family support	*2. Investigate whether this is affordable*	*2. FK*	*2. By next meeting*
	3. Intercultural training	*3. Organise intercultural training*	*3. JL*	*3. By May 2011*
3. New computer system (FY)	*Problems:* *1. More staff training needed* *2. System very slow sometimes*	*Hold meeting with computer system provider to identify solutions to both issues*	*FY to arrange meeting*	*asap*

Minutes of employee committee meeting held on 3 April 2011

Present: AB, JC, VD, FK, JL, FY   Apologies: MN

1. Communication in meetings

AB raised the following questions:

1. Are there too many meetings?
2. Are meetings run efficiently?

The meeting agreed to:

1. ....

2. streamline the procedures for meetings

AB ....

JC ....

Both actions ....

2. Foreign travel

JL requested:

1. special compensation for weekends away
2. family support
3. intercultural training

The meeting agreed that:

1. VD will ....
2. FK will .... at the next meeting
3. JL will ....

3. New computer system

....

....

....

....

Cultural note

In this unit, you have seen some techniques for streamlining your writing in order to make the process less time-consuming. Although time is based on measurable units (seconds, minutes, hours, days, etc.), not all cultures have the same attitude towards time. A distinction is made between **long-term orientation** and **short-term orientation**. In long-term oriented societies, people value actions and attitudes that affect the future. This is a reflection of the influence of Confucianism. Countries in this group include East-Asian cultures such as Korea, Japan, and China, where people tend to understand social interactions in the context of the long term.

Short-term-oriented societies are more directed towards the past and the present. In the West (Europe, USA, Canada), the objective of any transaction is to achieve the best give and take on that specific occasion. Therefore, an emphasis is placed on immediate gains – not on long-term benefits.

16 Editing for accuracy: Checking and correcting language

Proofread carefully to see if you any words out.[1] – Author unknown

Language covers the areas of:

1 grammar
2 vocabulary and expressions
3 spelling
4 sentence linking
5 sentence structure
6 sentence length

For language to be described as 'accurate', the writer must apply all of these language areas correctly.

Many writers try to achieve accuracy of language at the first draft. As discussed in Unit 15, this slows down the process of writing and forces the writer to concentrate on too many aspects at the same time. For example, if you are trying to decide on the appropriate content, structure, and style, as well as checking your language, you are likely to struggle. The result may be inefficient writing. Therefore, when working in a foreign language, it is especially important to have a procedure for writing. This will help you to write efficiently.

The following flow chart, first introduced in Unit 15, will remind you of a procedure for efficient writing:

1 Think about your readers

↓

2 Make a start: collect information

↓

3 Select the relevant information (concentrate on content)

↓

4 Write your first draft (concentrate on structure and style)

↓

5 Review and edit (concentrate on structure, style and language)

↓

6 Revise and write final draft (concentrate on all areas)

[1]Quote should read: 'Proofread carefully to see if you **have left** any words out.'

As the flow chart demonstrates, you should focus on editing your language in stages 5 and 6 – *after* you have written the first draft of your document. In this way, you can give your full concentration to your language.

Here are the main language points to check for when editing your document:

1 Grammar

- verb tenses
- agreement between subject and verb (e.g. use of 's' on third person singular of present tenses)
- prepositions
- adjectives and adverbs
- articles
- nouns (countable vs uncountable; capitalisation of proper nouns, etc.)

2 Vocabulary and expressions

- precise use of words
- missing words
- avoidance of repetition, (by using a thesaurus)
- use of key phrases (see Appendix 1)

3 Spelling

Use a spellchecker to identify basic mistakes. However, do not rely completely on a spellchecker, as English has many homophones (words which sound the same but are spelled differently and mean different things). For example, the following sentence is accepted by the spellchecker:

> ***Their*** *coming* ***too sea*** *if* ***its reel****.*

However, the writer is more likely to be trying to say:

> ***They're*** *coming* ***to see*** *if* ***it's real****.*

4 Sentence linking

Check that you have included suitable links between your sentences to make your writing flow. You can find more information on sentence linking in Unit 5.

5 Sentence structure

Check that you have used a variety of sentence structures: simple, compound, and complex. This will make your writing more interesting to read. You can find more information on sentence structure in Unit 6.

6 Sentence length

If in doubt, reduce the length of your longer sentences by creating some short simple sentences, especially for key information. You can find more information on sentence length in Unit 13.

Useful tips

- **When?** Edit your language *after* you have written your first draft.
- **How?** Concentrate on your grammar, vocabulary, spelling, and sentences (linking, structure, and length).
- **Why?** Check that your use of language is as accurate as possible.
- **How long?** Read through your document thoroughly at least once to check your language.
- Remember that your objective is to write a document which communicates your ideas or information in an effective way.

1 **The following extracts from business documents contain mistakes of grammar, spelling, and vocabulary. Correct the mistake in each line.**

1 Regarding your recent enquiry, we are pleased to inform you that the goods are now in stock and will be mailed out to your later today.

2 According with our records, we have not received payment for our invoice dated 11 September.

3 Our payment terms clearly state that payment is due within 30 days. Payment should therefore have been received until 12 October.

4 I am writing to confirm you the details of our next meeting, which will take place on 15 October at 14.00.

5 Could you please provide us with more informations about your requirements. We will then be able to respond in more detail.

6 Could you please explain more precisely what you mean with 'unexpected delay to our delivery'?

7 I regret inform that the goods you ordered will not be in stock until next month.

8 If I will hear nothing to the contrary, I shall assume that these terms are acceptable to you.

9 We hope that you will have no objections to change the delivery address.

10 I suggest to postpone the meeting until next month so that we can be sure that more of the project team will be available.

11 We would like to move forward with arranging a meeting. Therefore could you please get back to me as soon possible.

12 I can absolutely ensure you that the information will be treated in the strictest confidencee.

13 It is unlikely to have all the necessary information in time for the next meeting. Therefore I suggest we postpone the discussion till February.

14 I would like to congratulate you for passing the exam and wish you every success in your new position.

15 Do not hesitate to contact us again if you have any further question.

16 I look forward to hear from you as soon as you have read through the report.

2 **Edit the following document in terms of:**

- sentence linking
- sentence structure
- sentence length

Dear Mr Harrison

I wouild like to apply for the HR advisor position. It was advertised on your website.

I have two years' experience as an assistant in an international company in the food industry and worked in the central HR team and this has enabled me to develop know-how in recruitment and training and development, and I am currently supporting a company-wide project. This investigates the effectiveness of assessment centres.

I am pragmatic, dynamic, and independent, have a strong sense of creativity and have good organisational skills and am familiar with some office software. I am keen to learn to use other HR software tools. I believe that I would be an asset to your organisation. The assistant position would provide me with the ideal opportunity to develop my skills.

I would be delighted if you would like to meet me. Then we can discuss if my qualifications match the requirements for the position.

I have enclosed my résumé for your review. I hope that you will find it of interest.

I look forward to speaking to you.

Yours sincerely

Claire Martinez

Cultural note

Not all learners have the same attitude towards correctness. Is this difference a result of cultural background or personality variation? In other words, are some cultures more concerned about correctness than others?

It is clear that some cultures emphasise accuracy and precision, for example in terms of information, detail, promptness, and quality. They are less comfortable with vagueness and ambiguity. These cultures are generally **task-focused**. They like linear communication which gets straight to the point in a clear, precise, and accurate way. In contrast, there are cultures which are more **relationship-focused**. In relationship-focused cultures, there is less focus on accuracy and precision, and more on people: building trust and maintaining harmony.

17 Best practice 1: Emails

Email, instant messaging, and cell phones give us fabulous communication ability, but that communication is totally disorganized. – Marilyn vos Savant (American magazine columnist and author)

Throughout this book, you have followed two models for effective writing, based on:

1. **the elements of an effective document:**
   Content (Section 1)
   Structure (Section 2)
   Tone (Section 3)
   Language (Section 4)
2. **the steps for an efficient process (Section 5):**
   Write simply
   Write transparently
   Write quickly in order to produce your first draft
   Review and edit the language in order to produce your final draft

Now, in Section 6, we will shift focus to look at the differences in how you should communicate depending on the medium. First, let's look at the most common means of written communication – email.

Email has become the channel of choice for written business communication. It is:

- easy to write, with relatively few rules
- instant to send
- immediate to receive almost anywhere in the world.

As a result of its simplicity, some people in the business community say that email is an overused resource. For people who receive (and need to read) 100 or more emails a day, email is both a curse and a blessing.

To complement the units in this book on **writing** documents, the following table gives you some top tips to make sure your emails are **read**. However, it is important to consider these as tips and not as rules, since one of the defining features of email as a medium is its flexibility.

1 **Read each emailing tip, and decide if you adhere to it *always*, *sometimes* or *never*. Put a cross (X) in the relevant column.**

Top 10 Tips

	Always	Sometimes	Never
1 Use the subject field appropriately			
a Make the subject *relevant* to the topic of the email. In other words, if you are replying to an email and the subject has now moved on, reflect this change in the subject field.	☐	☐	☐
b Avoid treating the subject field as a greeting. 'Hello' is not useful in the subject field when the reader is looking through emails trying to find the one about the budget for the packaging project. Consider the subject field as the headline for your text.	☐	☐	☐
c Always fill the subject field – do not leave it blank.	☐	☐	☐
d Limit your subject field to 50 characters or less.	☐	☐	☐
e Keep it short. The best email subject lines are short, descriptive, and provide the reader with a reason to explore your message further.	☐	☐	☐
2 Quote the original email in your replies			
a Include the complete email. Do not cut the text of the original email to include only the relevant portions that you are replying to. Taking something out of context is often confusing, and emails are generally short enough for this not to be necessary.	☐	☐	☐
3 Make it easy for the reader to find your message			
a Write your response *above* the quoted text. Readers don't like having to scroll down just to find what you have written. Writers already know what they have written; and if they don't remember, they can scroll down to look.	☐	☐	☐
b Make your message as easy to read as possible. Use a font that is easy to read, and don't use too many colours – unusual colours and fonts will reduce the readability of your message.	☐	☐	☐
c Avoid sprinkling your replies in the middle of quoted text. This creates confusion when the exchange continues for more than a couple of emails.	☐	☐	☐
4 Use 'Reply', 'Reply (to) all', 'cc', and 'bcc' appropriately			
a Only use 'Reply to all' if you want your message to be seen by each person who received the original message and if you want to invite them to contribute to the discussion. Use only when you are *confident* that everyone will be interested in your response.	☐	☐	☐
b Use 'cc' sparingly: make sure you, as the writer, know why you are ccing someone into the email; and make sure the recipient in the cc field knows why they are receiving a copy of the message. Overuse can lead to confusion, as the recipient may not know if they are expected to act on the message; and also to inbox overload, as the recipient has to read the document.	☐	☐	☐
c Remember that 'bcc' is a useful function. Use 'bcc' (blind carbon copy) to tertiary recipients. Bcc recipients will receive the message without anyone else (including the 'to', 'cc', and 'bcc' recipients) seeing who the tertiary recipients are. It is common practice to use the 'bcc' field when addressing a very long list of recipients who do not need to (or who should not) know who else has been copied.	☐	☐	☐

	Always	Sometimes	Never
5 Use emoticons with caution			
a Avoid emoticons unless you are sure the recipient understands their meaning and their cultural significance. Tone is easy to mistake in emails and, while emoticons can help, in an international context they can very easily increase confusion.	☐	☐	☐
6 Be careful attaching files			
a Avoid attaching large files to the first email you send to someone.	☐	☐	☐
b Check with your recipient before sending large files.	☐	☐	☐
c Include attachments only when necessary and relevant. For example, graphic attachments, e.g. logos, take up space and are not necessary in every email.	☐	☐	☐
7 Know when to use abbreviations and acronyms – and when not to			
a Use commonly understood abbreviations and acronyms: these can help you to write clearly and concisely, but ...	☐	☐	☐
b Use acronyms for clarity and simplicity, not out of laziness. Don't fill your emails with acronyms like OTOH (on the other hand), EOD (end of day) and AFAIK (as far as I know). If you're too busy to spell something out in your message, send it when you have more time to write in full. Messages like 'Pete, AFAIK, the report is due EOD. HTH. BFN' ('Pete, as far as I know, the report is due at the end of the day. Hope that helps. Bye for now.') are difficult to read and best left to text-messaging teenagers.	☐	☐	☐
8 Answer quickly			
a Reply to all emails within 24 hours (preferably within the same working day).	☐	☐	☐
b If an email is complicated and requires more thought or work, reply to the sender saying that you have received their email and giving the date by which you will get back to them.	☐	☐	☐
9 Avoid using email to send personal or confidential information			
a Be aware that sending confidential information by email is dangerous. Email is not a secure method of communication; in addition, in an open working environment, emails can easily be accessed by others who are not intended readers.	☐	☐	☐
b Keep personal information out of emails. Including personal information that you do not want to be publicly known can lead to trouble.	☐	☐	☐
c Protect confidential information sent by email by using secure encryption.	☐	☐	☐
10 Use a disclaimer			
a Include a disclaimer in all external emails to help protect your company from legal liability. For example, if an employee accidentally forwards a virus to a customer by email, the customer may decide to sue your company for damages. If you add a disclaimer at the bottom of every external mail, saying that the recipient must check each email for viruses, this can be used in court to avoid liability.	☐	☐	☐

2 **The purpose of the previous exercise was to get you to evaluate your own writing by indicating whether you are in the habit of using each tip:**

- **always**
- **sometimes**
- **never**

List below three of the tips that you think are important and that you are confident you *always* remember to use:

1 ....

2 ....

3 ....

Now list three tips that you *sometimes* use, but which are not always part of your established practice for writing emails. How are you going to change your email writing practice to integrate these tips?

1 ....

2 ....

3 ....

Finally, list three tips that you *never* use. Why do you not apply these tips to your writing? Do you think you should try to in the future?

1 ....

2 ....

3 ....

Cultural note

The emergence of email as the main channel for written communication has led to a search for standards. At an international and intercultural level, two questions arise:

1 Is it possible to have agreed international standards for emails?

2 Is it important for the future development of emails to have agreed standards?

In order to answer these questions, one needs to think about the cultural differences between standardisation and adaptation. In other words, it is important to recognise the distinction between:

- cultures where people are more comfortable with a set of standardised practices. Such cultures, whose members seek certainty in accepted rules, are commonly termed **risk-avoidance cultures**. They look for standardised approaches for activities, including email writing.
- cultures where people are more comfortable finding their own way of doing things, without having them imposed by external rules. Members of these cultures, commonly termed **risk-embracing cultures**, do not need the certainty of accepted rules. They are comfortable with flexible practices, and are more open to adaptation and innovation.

18 Best practice 2: Business reports

This report, by its very length, defends itself against the risk of being read.
– Winston Churchill (British Prime Minister, 1940–45 and 1951–55)

A business report is a document which reaches conclusions and offers recommendations. These recommendations may be for the solution of a problem or a proposal for future action. Before making these recommendations, the report writer carries out:

- a thorough study
- a collection of all relevant facts and information
- a detailed analysis

After this, the report writer reaches a conclusion. The conclusion is supported by:

- statements
- other relevant data

These conclusions then lead to the suggested next steps – the recommendations.

There are many types of business report. Here are just a few:

- general business report
- business plan
- business proposal
- marketing plan
- strategic plan
- business analysis
- project report
- project review
- financial plan

Although these reports are all different, the report-writing process will be essentially the same.

1 Structure

A report is a tool that helps people make decisions by giving them data in a structured way. A business report has a linear structure. It moves in an organised way through a series of steps. The typical structure of a report is:

1. Title page
2. Table of contents (or TOC)
3. Executive summary
4. Introduction/Background
5. Main body
6. Conclusions and recommendations

7 Recommendations
8 Appendices

2 Visuals

Visuals can be used to make reports more effective. Here are some ideas of types of visuals:

- tables
- pie charts
- line charts
- bar charts
- timelines
- others, such as pictograms, maps, and flow charts

Here are some important reasons for using visuals:

- to arouse reader interest
- to emphasise key information
- to summarise a large quantity of information
- to simplify concepts
- to help non-native readers

3 Reader engagement

Finally, where should you place your energies when developing your skills? The following table shows which parts of a business report are likely to be read by the average executive. This can also guide you as to where you should place the emphasis for your future development.

Part of report	Will the executive read it?
1 Title page	Always
2 Table of contents	Always
3 Executive summary	Always
4 Introduction	Sometimes
5 Main body	If interested in data and findings
6 Conclusions and recommendations	Nearly always
7 Appendices	Rarely

1 **Elements a–k are from a business report. Match each element with the section that you would expect to find it in. Write your answers in the table.**

a Main arguments and options

b Detailed evidence

c The authors

d Outline of the context of the report

e Summary of findings

f Part of the report showing where to find information

g Suggested next steps

h Additional information

i Short version of the complete report in one or two paragraphs

j The date of publication

k Detailed data

Report section	Report element
1 Title page	
2 Table of contents (or TOC)	
3 Executive summary	
4 Introduction/Background	
5 Main body	
6 Conclusions	
7 Recommendations	
8 Appendices	

4 The stages of writing a good report

Business reports are essential documents as they provide information on how an organisation is performing. Therefore, good report-writing skills are vital in the business environment. However, reports are often:

- too long
- poorly written
- boring to read

The result is that, even when the content of the report is important, it is unlikely to be fully read. So, what can you, as a writer, do to increase the chances that your report will be read?

The key stages in the report-writing process are:

1 Preparing
2 Writing the first draft
3 Editing and producing the final version.

2 **Look at the key stages from the writing process listed on the previous page. Now use what you have learned in earlier units about efficient writing to match the tasks shown below with the relevant stage of the process. Write your answers in the table.**

a check if there is any redundant information

b write briefly, simply, and quickly

c write the Table of contents

d make sure what type of report is required

e use diagrams and pictures wherever possible

f write the Executive summary

g check that my document is easy to navigate

h make a plan

i check that my document is written in correct language (spelling, grammar, and vocabulary)

j choose language that is easy to read

k carry out initial research

l check that the report is divided into short paragraphs of between two and six sentences

Report stage	Report task
1 Preparing	
2 Writing the first draft	
3 Editing and producing the final version	

Cultural note

Central to the model of the business report presented in this unit is rational argument. It is based on the type of thinking that developed in the west, which came from Greek philosophy. The Greek culture placed great emphasis on:

- the use of language
- the creation of categories, and
- the value of debate

in order to reach conclusions.

However, this practice is not universal; other cultures have different approaches. Consider the following contrast:

– Western cultures consider **opposing views** in order to reach conclusions; they use a process of debate, which evaluates differences and finally reaches a result. This is the basis for the report model in this unit.

– Eastern cultures, in contrast, resolve differences by looking for commonalities. This method achieves results through **harmonising opposites**.

Therefore, the challenge for report writers in an international context is to find a model which is comprehensible in different cultural settings.

19 Best practice 3: Minutes

Minutes are primarily written for people who were at the meeting, not for people who were not! – Anon

Minutes are the **written record** of a meeting. The document usually gives:

- date, time, and place of the meeting
- a list of those present
- apologies for absence for those not present
- approval of the previous meeting's minutes
- matters arising: a report on the discussion of issues arising from the minutes of the previous meeting
- for each item on the agenda, a record of the principal points discussed and decisions taken
- AOB (Any Other Business): a record of any discussion of items not listed on the agenda
- time, date, and place of the next meeting
- name of the person taking the minutes

In fact, there are two entirely separate documents created for a minuted meeting – the notes and the minutes. Notes are usually written during the meeting by the *minute-taker* or *secretary*, though sometimes, they are audio-recorded. They are then *written up* into minutes, *filed* for future reference, and *circulated* to the meeting *participants* and other interested parties. However, they are primarily written for the people who:

- attended the meeting
- apologised for their absence

Minutes are important because they show:

- what was decided in the meeting
- what was achieved in the meeting
- what was agreed in terms of next steps (action items)

Without minutes, time is wasted trying to remember what was covered in the previous meeting.

To be effective, minutes must be:

- brief (a summary – not a word-for-word account)
- relevant (record important information, especially decisions and next steps)

The key stages for the minute-taker are:

1 before the meeting (preparing)
2 during the meeting (taking notes)
3 after the meeting (writing up the minutes)

First look at some of the tasks for each of these stages:

1 Before the meeting

- read the agenda
- check with the chair of the meeting if anything on the agenda is not clear

2 During the meeting

- listen
- summarise the discussion
- take notes of the decisions and next steps
- use appropriate language, especially vocabulary
- report what was said (see Appendix 3 for a list of 'reporting verbs')

3 After the meeting

- write up a first draft from your notes
- edit the first draft (focus on content – brevity and relevance)
- ask the chair if any items are not clear
- proof read the first draft (focus on language – accuracy and tone)
- produce the final draft
- file the minutes for future reference, and circulate them if appropriate

A form such as the one below can be used for taking notes before and during the meeting. Go to Appendix 4 for a full-sized version of the form that you can use for your own note-taking.

Date: Time: Place:	Present:		Apologies for absence:	
Discussion at the meeting		**Required follow-up after the meeting**		
Agenda item	**Discussion**	**Action (WHAT)**	**Person responsible (WHO)**	**Timeframe/ Deadline (WHEN)**
1. Matters arising:				

1 **Now look at the additional tasks listed below. At which stage does each task come for the minute-taker? The stages are:**

1 before the meeting

2 during the meeting

3 after the meeting

Write 1, 2, or 3 in the right-hand column.

Tasks	Stage
a Check that the minutes follow the order of points on the agenda.	
b Note down a summary of the major points raised.	
c Check that the minutes give each point a separate paragraph.	
d Make a map of the seating so that I know the names of the participants and where they are sitting.	
e Distribute the agenda so that participants can prepare for the meeting.	
f Distribute the minutes.	
g Edit the first draft – preferably within 48 hours – to improve language and tone.	
h Read through the minutes of the last meeting.	
i File the minutes so that they can be easily found for future reference.	
j Make a note of those present and those absent.	
k Check that the minutes state, for each point, the main issues, decisions taken and next steps.	
l Prepare an outline for the minutes based on the agenda and leave space for notes.	
m Get the approval of the chair that the minutes are correct.	
n Think where you are going to sit in relation to the chair and other participants.	
o Write up the first draft of the minutes – preferably within 24 hours.	

2 **Below are ten quotes from a business meeting. Imagine that you are the minute-taker for the meeting. Make yourself a copy of the form on page 77 (or go to Appendix 4 for a full-size version) and then write your notes, based on the quotes below, into the relevant boxes in the form.**

1 'Okay, let's get started. I'm afraid that Pete Bartlett can't be with us this afternoon, as he has had to meet a client.'

2 'Can we now move on to the second item on the agenda: staff recruitment?'

3 'I've received one item of Other Business: project planning software.'

4 'Thanks, everyone, for your input. To summarise, three of us are in favour of recruiting a new trainee.'

5 'Does 4 July suit everyone for our next meeting?'

6 'John, can you please prepare the job specification for the trainee position?'

7 'It seems that 4 July is not convenient for everyone. How about a week later? That's 11 July. 9 o'clock start.'

8 'OK, let's start with the action from last month's meeting: additional office space. I believe that this has now been resolved.'

9 John: 'No problem. I'll work on it next week. And I'll circulate the document by 15 June.'

10 'Let's hold the next meeting in the Boardroom – it's bigger than here, and more comfortable.'

Cultural note

It is universally agreed that the aim of minutes is to provide a record of a meeting so that it can achieve its highest potential. So, why is it sometimes the case that minute-takers fail to circulate the minutes in a timely manner? Or those who agreed to take on follow-up tasks fail to deliver on time?

It is clear that multi-tasking is becoming more important in the modern business environment, as staff are asked to take on more tasks with ever-shorter deadlines. Perhaps it is not surprising then that, for some, the additional tasks agreed to in the heat of the meeting are overtaken by other priorities. Hence the need for minutes to:

- back up decisions
- maintain a record of decisions and discussions
- help everyone stay on track

20 Best practice 4: Business writing

Every writer I know has trouble writing. – Joseph Heller (American novelist, short story writer. and playwright)

The following self-assessment questionnaire is intended to help you discover how good your business writing practice is. First, answer the questions below by putting a cross (X) in the relevant column.

The questionnaire is divided into five sections:

1 Content
2 Structure
3 Tone
4 Language
5 Writing the first draft; then editing it and producing the final version

These five sections reflect the key themes of this book.

1

1 Content *Before starting to write, I ask myself …*	Always	Usually	Sometimes	Rarely	Never	
a what my reader already knows about the subject.	☐	☐	☐	☐	☐	Unit 1
b how much information the reader needs to know about the subject.	☐	☐	☐	☐	☐	Unit 1
c how I can present the information in a concise way.	☐	☐	☐	☐	☐	Unit 1
d what is the appropriate technical level for my reader(s).	☐	☐	☐	☐	☐	Unit 2
e if there is too much or too little detail.	☐	☐	☐	☐	☐	Unit 2
2 Structure *When writing, I …*						
a break up my document into meaningful sections.	☐	☐	☐	☐	☐	Units 4, 13, 14
b use paragraphs, headings, lists, and bold type to make the document easier to read.	☐	☐	☐	☐	☐	Units 3, 4, 13

	Always	Usually	Sometimes	Rarely	Never	
c use linking words and phrases to show the relationships between my ideas and information.	☐	☐	☐	☐	☐	Unit 5
d use a variety of sentence structures and sentence lengths to make my writing more interesting and engaging.	☐	☐	☐	☐	☐	Units 5, 6, 9, 13
3 Tone *When writing, I ...*						
a choose language appropriate to the relationship with my reader(s).	☐	☐	☐	☐	☐	Units 7, 8
b choose a tone that is appropriate to the subject of the message.	☐	☐	☐	☐	☐	Units 7, 8
4 Language *When writing, I ...*						
a start by specifying the purpose of my document.	☐	☐	☐	☐	☐	Unit 10
b use clear language in order to make my document easy to read.	☐	☐	☐	☐	☐	Unit 11
c bring my document to a transparent end so that my reader knows the next steps.	☐	☐	☐	☐	☐	Unit 12
5 Writing the first draft, editing the first draft, and producing the final version *When writing my first draft, I ...*						
a write briefly and concisely	☐	☐	☐	☐	☐	Unit 13
b write transparently	☐	☐	☐	☐	☐	Unit 14
c write quickly	☐	☐	☐	☐	☐	Unit 15
After writing my first draft, I check ...						
d if there is too much or too little detail.	☐	☐	☐	☐	☐	Unit 1
e if there is any redundant information.	☐	☐	☐	☐	☐	Unit 1
f that my document has a transparent external structure.	☐	☐	☐	☐	☐	Units 3, 4, 14
g that my document has a clear internal structure and development.	☐	☐	☐	☐	☐	Units 5, 6
h that my document is written in an appropriate tone.	☐	☐	☐	☐	☐	Units 7, 8, 9
i that my document is written in correct language (grammar and vocabulary).	☐	☐	☐	☐	☐	Units 11,16
Points	**x 5**	**x 4**	**x 3**	**x 2**	**x 1**	

Now you can check your overall score. For every cross (X):

- in the 'always' column, you score 5 points =
- in the 'usually' column, you score 4 points =
- in the 'sometimes' column, you score 3 points =
- in the 'rarely' column, you score 2 points =
- in the 'never' column, you score 1 point =

Now add your points together. **Total** [ ]

How to interpret your score.

105–115:
You have a very good knowledge of the elements of business writing in terms of content, structure, tone, and language; you also know the importance of reviewing your documents.
90–104:
You have a good knowledge of the elements of business writing; however you need to focus more on specific elements of business writing – either in terms of the process of writing/reviewing or on the final document. Look at your lowest scores in order to identify any specific weaknesses that you would like to work on.
70–89:
You have a basic knowledge of the elements of business writing; however, you need to place more energy on both the process of writing and on the final written document. Choose three areas of weakness that you need to work on and review the relevant units.
55–69:
You need to spend more time both on writing and on reviewing in order to develop a better process for writing and create better final written documents. Choose five areas of weakness that you need to work on and review the relevant units.
Below 55:
You need to gain a clearer understanding of the elements of business writing in terms of the process of writing and the final written documents. You should choose eight areas from the book that you would like to concentrate on.

2 **The purpose of the self-assessment questionnaire is to identify:**

- **strengths, i.e. those areas where you scored high points**
- **weaknesses, i.e. those areas where you scored low points**

List below three strengths. These are areas which you feel comfortable with:

1 ....

2 ....

3 ....

Now list three weaknesses. These are areas where you need further development:

1 ....

2 ....

3 ....

Finally, list the units in *English for Business: Writing* which you aim to review:

1 ....

2 ....

3 ....

Cultural note

Feedback is one of the ways that we find out about how we are performing. It provides us with information about our strengths and weaknesses. When feedback is delivered in an appropriate manner, it can be a powerful force for both personal and professional development. But what is 'an appropriate manner'? There is a difference between those cultures which celebrate success and those which downplay it.

In cultures which celebrate success, the idea is that you motivate people to do better by giving them positive feedback. In other words, success creates more success. The positive circle starts with a pat on the back or words of praise. This makes the listener feel good. This leads to increased self-confidence, which, in turn leads to higher performance. However, not all cultures have the same attitude towards **positive feedback**. In some cultures, **negative feedback**, which highlights mistakes, is seen as the way to develop. In other words, the road to improvement lies in understanding one's weaknesses and taking action to overcome them.

APPENDIX 1 – Key phrases for business letters and emails

1. Greetings

Dear (+ first name)

Dear Mr / Ms (+ surname)

Dear Sir / Madam (*British English*)

Ladies and gentlemen (*American English*)

Hello / Hi (+first name) (*informal*)

2. Introduction / reference / purpose

Introduction

You may recall that we met last week ... In the course of the conversation you mentioned ...

I recently read your article / advertisement ...

I was given your name by [name] ... who suggested that ...

Reference

Thank you for your letter / email / message of [date] concerning / about / enclosing / enquiring ...

I have received your letter / email of [date] ...

Further to / With regard to / Regarding / With reference to ...

On the subject of ...

In terms of ...

In response to ...

According to my records, ...

Re your email ...

I am pleased / sorry to hear / learn that ...

I note that ...

Purpose

I am writing to request / enquire / inform / check / confirm / ask ...

Just a quick email to ...

Sometimes it is appropriate to write a social phrase, similar to an expression that would be used in a face-to-face meeting.

Social openings

How are you?

How's life?

How're things?

What's the weather like? It's awful / terrible / depressing here. It's great / beautiful / marvellous here. It's sunny / really hot / bitterly cold.

3. Main part

The precise phrases will, of course, depend on the purpose of the email. Below are the key phrases for some typical purposes. In addition, these key phrases can be used at the beginning of paragraphs to signal your intentions. For more information on signalling intentions, see Unit 11.

Requesting

I would be grateful if you could ...

I would appreciate it if you could ...

Could you please send / supply / confirm ...

Please send / supply / confirm ...

Informing

I am pleased to inform you ...

I would like to inform you ...

I am now in a position to inform you / confirm ...

Expressing wishes

I would (very much) like to place the following order / organise a meeting ...

I (particularly) want to ...

I (do) hope ...

I require / need ...

It would be great to ...

I would prefer not to ...

I would rather not ...

I am reluctant to ...

Asking for clarification

It is not clear whether ...

I am not sure if ...

Could you clarify / supply us with more information ...

Am I right in thinking ... ?

Could you please explain what you mean by ... ?

Offering

I can / am able to / would like to offer you / provide you with ...

If you wish, I would be happy to ...

Would you like me to ...

Shall I ...

Do you want me to ...

Providing documentation

I am enclosing / attaching ...

I enclose / attach ...

Please find enclosed / attached ...

Confirming

If I hear nothing to the contrary, I shall assume that ...

I hereby confirm ...

I am able / pleased to confirm ...

Drawing attention and reminding

I would like to point out ...

May I draw your attention to ...

Please note that ...

Agreeing

I am willing to ...

I agree to ...

I am happy to ...

... is acceptable / fine.

Disagreeing and refusing requests

Unfortunately, I am unable to ...

I am unwilling to ...

I cannot agree with / to that ...

Asking for approval

We hope that [our solution] will be to your satisfaction / meet with your approval.

We hope that you will have no objections to ...

Making suggestions

I propose / suggest that ...

I would (strongly) advise / recommend ....

It is advisable ...

You might consider ...

Might I suggest that ...

Expressing urgency and necessity

I should like to remind you ...

It is obligatory / necessary for ...

You are obliged (by law) to / It is required (by law) to ...

You must / have to ...

It is of the utmost importance that ...

On no account ...

Under no circumstances ...

It is important / vital / essential ...

... at your earliest convenience.

... as soon as possible.

... without further delay.

... by return of post.

... by Friday / the end of January

Giving good news

I am delighted to inform you / hear that ...

You will be delighted to hear that ...

You'll be happy to hear that ...

Giving bad news

I regret to inform you that ...

Unfortunately, ...

I am afraid ...

I'm sorry but ...

Expressing disappointment

I was disappointed to hear your decision ...

I am very sorry that you feel that / unable to ...

Apologising

I am / was sorry to hear / learn that ...

I apologise for ...

Please accept our apologies for ...

I regret that ...

Refusing politely

I (fully) appreciate your point of view / difficulties but ...

I'm afraid that we are not in a position to ...

Regretfully, I have to inform you that ...

We realise this is not ideal. However, ...

Threatening

If you do not ..., I shall ...

Unless you ..., I shall ... be forced to place the matter in the hands or our lawyers.

Giving assurance

I assure you / give you my assurance that ...

You may rest assured that ...

I shall / will do my utmost to ensure that ...

Expressing need for confidentiality

Please treat this as strictly confidential / in the strictest confidence.

I should be grateful if you would handle this matter with discretion.

Guaranteeing confidentiality / discretion

Any information will be treated as strictly confidential.

The matter will be handled with discretion.

Acknowledging actions and instructions

I note that you have ...

I have received / taken delivery of ...

I note that I must ...

Reminding

May I remind you ...

I would like to remind you ...

Just to remind you ...

Don't forget to ...

Expressing confidence and hope

We are confident that ...

We trust / hope that you will ...

We expect / anticipate / forecast / think / envisage / believe ...

Expressing certainty, probability, possibility, improbability, impossibility

It is certain that ...

There is no doubt that ...

I am confident that ...

It is likely / probable / possible that ...

There is some doubt as to whether ...

It is unlikely that ...

It is impossible for us to ...

Congratulating

I would like to take this opportunity to congratulate you on ...

I would like to congratulate you on ...

Congratulations on ...

4. Next steps

What

The next steps are as follows:

The plan for the next phase is:

We expect to move forward as follows:

We are now in a position to ...

Who

Therefore I would be grateful if you could ...

Could you please confirm that you can ...

We would appreciate if you could ...

When

The deadline for receiving the information is ...

The timetable for project completion is ...

We would like to finish this phase by ...

We must / have to / need to finish / complete ... by ...

5. Pre-closing

Offering further assistance

Do not hesitate to contact us again if you require further assistance.

If you have any further questions, please contact me.

Let me know if you need any more help.

Please contact me if I can be of further assistance.

Friendly sign-off

I look forward to meeting / seeing you next week / in January.

I am looking forward to meeting / seeing you ...

I look forward to / I am looking forward to hearing from you.

I look forward to receiving your report ...

I am looking forward to receiving your order ...

Looking forward to ...

See you ...

Final thanks

Thanking you in advance.

Thank you once again for your assistance.

Thank you for your understanding in this matter.

6. Farewell

Yours faithfully

Yours sincerely

(Best) regards

Best

Best wishes

Notes

The greeting and the farewell are usually linked, as follows:

Dear (first name), Hello (first name), Hi (first name)
Best, Best wishes, (Best) Regards

Dear Mr / Ms (+ surname) (*British English*)
Yours sincerely

Dear Sir / Madam (*British English*)
Yours faithfully

Ladies and gentlemen (*American English*)
Yours sincerely

7. Social phrases for emails

Questions / Comments

How are you?

How's life?

How're things?

Hope you're not overworking!

Long time no hear.

Hope life is treating you well.

Greetings from sunny England / France / Germany / Sweden ...

Greetings from rainy Italy / Spain / Greece.

What's the weather like over there?

It's awful / terrible / depressing here.

It's great / beautiful / marvellous here.

It's sunny / really hot / bitterly cold.

Answers / Comments

We are very busy here at the moment.

I've just returned from my holidays and I'm still catching up.

I'm going away next week, so there's a lot to do.

APPENDIX 2 – Linking words and phrases

Addition

also • in addition • too • as well

Alternation

instead • alternatively

Cause

therefore • so • consequently • thus

Comparison

similarly • in the same way • likewise

Concession

anyway • at any rate

Conclusion

in conclusion • finally • lastly

Condition

then • in that case

Contradiction

in fact • actually • as a matter of fact

Contrast

yet • however • but • nevertheless

Equivalence

in other words • that means • namely • that is to say

Example

for example • for instance

Generalisation

usually/normally • as a rule • in general

Highlight

in particular • especially

Inclusion

for example • for instance • such as • as follows

Counter-evidence

on the other hand • conversely

Stating the obvious

obviously • naturally • of course

Summary

to sum up • overall • in brief/short

APPENDIX 3 – Reporting verbs

Sample sentences

1 G&D <u>have promised to deliver</u> by the end of the month.
2 The CEO <u>admitted that</u> it had been a tough year.
3 The Finance Director <u>suggested reducing</u> the budget by 2%.
4 The Marketing Director <u>presented her new proposals</u>.
5 The new boss <u>instructed the staff to attend</u> a meeting at 8 o'clock.
6 The chairman of the board <u>assured shareholders that</u> the company would show a profit the following year.

Form

The sample sentences on the left are examples of six common constructions that you find with verbs for reporting:

1 verb + infinitive with 'to'
2 verb + 'that' clause *
3 verb + '-ing' form
4 verb + object (only)
5 verb + object + infinitive with 'to'
6 verb + object + 'that' clause *

* The word 'that' can sometimes be omitted.

Uses

Here are some reporting verbs and the constructions they take:

	1	2	3	4	5	6
add		•		•		
admit		•	•	•		
agree	•	•				
announce		•		•		
answer		•		•		
argue		•				
assure						•
authorise				•	•	
believe		•		•		
claim	•	•				
comment		•				
confirm		•		•		
consent	•					
consider		•	•	•		
declare		•				
decline	•			•		
demand	•	•		•		
deny		•	•	•		
describe				•		
disclose		•		•		
emphasise		•		•		
estimate		•		•		
explain		•		•		
forecast		•		•		

	1	2	3	4	5	6
guess		•		•		
indicate		•		•		
inform						•
invite					•	
maintain		•		•		
outline				•		
notify						•
predict		•		•		
present				•		
presume		•				
promise	•	•		•	•	•
propose	•	•	•	•		
prove		•		•		
recommend		•	•	•	•	
refuse	•			•		
reply		•				
report		•		•		
require		•	•	•	•	
say		•		•		
state		•		•		
stress		•		•		
suggest		•	•	•		
tell				•	•	•
threaten	•	•		•		

APPENDIX 4 – Sample documents

The following pages show emails and letters linked to meetings. They follow the steps before and after a meeting and include:

- invitation to a meeting (informal email)
- offering availability (informal email)
- invitation to a meeting (formal letter)
- apologies for absence (informal email)
- apologies for absence (formal email)
- confirmation of attendance (neutral)
- confirmation of meeting and request for agenda items (informal)
- postponing / rescheduling of the meeting (neutral)
- sending out the minutes (neutral)
- reminders about outstanding actions (neutral)
- apology for late completion of outstanding action (neutral)

They demonstrate the difference between informal, neutral and formal tones of writing.

In addition, you will find:

- a sample report to be read before a meeting
- sample agendas for informal and formal meetings
- template for writing notes during a meeting
- sample notes written during a meeting
- minutes document written using the notes

Email invitation to a meeting (informal)

To: Management London

Subject: Quarterly meeting

Dear all

We need to fix a time for our quarterly meeting. In the past, we have allocated 3 hours to go through the agenda. This quarter, because of the number of major issues to address, I think we will need a little longer. I am attaching a draft agenda and would like to have your thoughts on the timing for these items.

We normally schedule the meeting for the last week of June. For this meeting, I propose an afternoon session, starting at 13.30. Could you please get back to me asap with your availability and feedback on the timing for the agenda items.

Finally, I am attaching the report on training, staff development and career development prepared by the Staff Development Team. Please ensure that you have read it before the meeting so that we can start to identify solutions. See point 3 on the agenda.

Regards

Peter

Draft agenda (informal)

Agenda

Quarterly meeting: date to be confirmed

Matters arising

1. **Directors' bonuses**
   – new basis for calculation
   – payment schedule
2. **IT infrastructure**
   – plans
   – investment
   – scheduling
3. **Training, staff development and career development**
   – discussion of report findings
   – next steps
4. **Shared services**
   – departmental mergers
   – staff issues
   – team meetings

AOB

Report on training, staff development and career development

TRAINING, STAFF DEVELOPMENT AND CAREER DEVELOPMENT

A. Introduction

This is the second report produced by the Staff Development Team, which we set up in 2008 as part of our initiative to implement a staff development plan. The purpose of the report is to consolidate the developmental feedback gained from the employee survey carried out during the autumn into training, staff development and career development.

B. General points

Training:

Employees felt, in general, that although there was a commitment to training, the company had very little to offer in terms of staff development and career progression. In particular:

- Few staff had received formal training despite the changes to their work roles.
- Most staff experienced practical obstacles to obtaining the training they felt they needed.
- The biggest obstacles were reduced funding for training, spending priorities and the lack of time to undertake training.

Further qualifications:

- Several members of staff were studying for further qualifications which they did largely in their own time and at their own expense.

Staff development:

- Most administrative and support staff did not feel that the company was committed to staff development.

Career progression:

- Staff expressed most frustration over their opportunities for career progression within the organization. In particular:
- The majority felt that they had no opportunities for progression at all.
- They identified the structure of the company and lack of funding as the major constraints on their career progression.
- Many believed that the only way to progress was to move outside the company.

C. Specific comments

The following comments represent some of the key issues raised by employees:

'... when I was appointed ... I was offered no training at all, so it was up to me to go and find it, which I did. But then they paid for it ... they were fine.'

' We are encouraged to go, but I want to do a computer technicians' course, and the cost is so high ... There is encouragement to do it provided it doesn't cost too much.'

'I think it's very difficult for us to justify commercial courses, costing over a thousand [pounds] for a few days, [even though they're better courses] ...

'I think managers are scared to send you on training courses, because it means you're going to want new technology, you're going to want new services, that are going on in that training course.'

'... the facilities are available, there are courses put on ... but I do not have the time to go.'

'When I came into the firm I didn't have any qualifications. I felt I had to have them, you know, to be on a level ... to justify my existence I had to have qualifications, and ... I actually feel it makes me able to do my job.'

'I think the way the structure is built up is wrong in a sense. There's no middle tier that you could move up to slowly, climb up and climb up ... It's a very steep pyramid.'

D. Recommendations

We recommend that we separate the issues so that we can address them in a more consistent way. The points fall into the following main categories:

1. opportunities for training
2. obstacles in training provision
3. training for qualifications
4. commitment to staff development
5. formal procedures for staff development
6. opportunities for career progression
7. obstacles to career progression

We propose that these 7 areas be put onto the agenda of the next quarterly meeting so that we can start to define solutions.

Email offering availability for a meeting (neutral)

To: peter.ford@tribetech.com

Subject: RE: Quarterly meeting

Dear Peter

Thanks for your email and the documentation for our quarterly meeting.

I am available on the following dates in the afternoon:
24 June
25 June
27 June

I propose the following timings for the agenda items:
1. Directors' bonuses (90 minutes)
2. IT infrastructure (45 minutes)
3. Training, staff development and career development (60 minutes)
4. Shared services (45 minutes)

Regards

Jeremy

Apologies for absence at meeting (informal)

To: peter.ford@tribetech.com
Subject: Staff committee meeting
Hi Peter I'm afraid that I won't be able to make tomorrow's staff committee meeting. Something important has come up here in Dubai and I will need to resolve it before I come back to the UK. I will be back in time for the quarterly meeting in the last week of June. Sorry I couldn't give you more notice. Regards Shafiq

Confirmation of attendance at meeting (neutral)

To: peter.ford@tribetech.com
Subject: RE: Agenda
Dear Peter Thank you for sending me the agenda for the forthcoming meeting. I confirm that 27 June at 14.00 is OK for me. In your email, you asked for additional points for the agenda. I would be grateful if you could add an item on 'Environmental initiatives'. I look forward to seeing you on 27 June. Regards Murray

Apologies for absence at meeting (formal)

To: k.p.appleby@tribetech.com
Subject: RE: IT Rollout Meeting
Dear Mr Appleby Thank you for sending me the details of the forthcoming IT Rollout Meeting for the Asia Pacific Region. I regret to inform you that I will be on annual leave at the time of the meeting and will, therefore, not be able to attend. Yours sincerely Francis K Stormont

Confirmation of meeting and request for agenda items (informal)

To: Marketing All
Subject: Marketing meeting confirmation and agenda
Dear all Thanks for sending me details of your availability in April for a marketing meeting. I confirm that the meeting will take place on 18 April at 09.00 in my office. I am attaching the latest version of the agenda. If you have any further items to add, please let me know asap. See you all then. Regards Julie

Postponing/rescheduling of the meeting (neutral)

To: International Sales Department
Subject: RE: April meeting
Dear team members Thanks for sending me details of your availability in April for a face-to-face project review meeting. It seems that April will not be possible because of various international work commitments. Therefore the April meeting will need to be rescheduled. Could you please let me know your availability for a face-to-face team meeting in May. Thanks and regards Thi

Sending out the minutes (neutral)

To: Command Project Group
Subject: Follow-up from last week's meeting
Dear all Thanks for your participation at last week's meeting. As we all know, virtual meetings can be difficult because of time differences, technology issues and diversity challenges. But I'm sure you'll agree that Manfred did an excellent job as facilitator; and I was particularly pleased with the level of contributions from all of us all around the world. I am attaching the minutes with this email. Please read through them. If there are questions about the content or about your follow-up tasks, please contact me. Regards Saphyra

Reminder about outstanding actions (neutral)

To: helen@commandproject.com
Subject: Overdue work
Dear Helen I'm writing to remind you about the follow-up action after our last meeting that you agreed to take on: supplier analysis. The due date for me to receive your analysis was the end of last week. Please could you let me know when I can expect your report? If you would like to discuss the task, feel free to contact me. Regards Artur

Further reminder about outstanding actions (neutral)

To: helen@commandproject.com
Subject: RE: Overdue work
Dear Helen I'm disappointed not to have heard from you after my last email, reminding you about the agreed follow-up: supplier analysis. I would appreciate if you could give me a call before the end of the week to let me know when I can expect your report. Regards Artur

If Artur has not had a response after two email reminders, he should call Helen.

Apology for late completion of outstanding action (informal)

To: artur@commandproject.com
Subject: RE: RE: Overdue work
Hi Artur I'm very sorry about the delay in getting the supplier analysis to you. I've been really busy with end-of-quarter figures. But, we've now completed the quarterly tasks and I promise that you will have the analysis by next Wednesday. Sorry again for the delay. Hope you understand. Best wishes Helen

Letter of invitation to a meeting (formal)

PRC Hammerslow

15 November 2011

Dear member

PRC HAMMERSLOW BRANCH ANNUAL GENERAL MEETING

You are invited to the PRC Branch Annual General Meeting on **Tuesday 18 February 2012 at 16.00** at The Civic Centre in Hammerslow (see enclosed map).

An agenda is enclosed together with a form for nomination of officers and a form for submitting motions. Completed forms should be returned to me by Tuesday 11 February 2012.

As well as dealing with elections, the AGM will be an opportunity to find out more about what the group has been doing over the last year and to make plans for the coming year. There will also be plenty of time to discuss issues which concern you.

There will be an invited speaker, who will present current campaigns and this will be a useful opportunity to find out how matters are progressing. It will also give you a chance to have your say about what you think should happen next. After the meeting there will be a social event. All members are invited to this.

If you would like further information, including details of disabled access, please contact me at the above telephone number. I look forward to seeing you on 18 February.

Best wishes

John Smith
PRC Hammerslow Branch Secretary

Agenda for an AGM (formal)

PRC HAMMERSLOW BRANCH ANNUAL GENERAL MEETING
TUESDAY 18 FEBRUARY 2012
The Civic Centre, Hammerslow

Agenda

Welcome by the chair

Apologies for absence

Minutes of previous AGM and matters arising

Chair's report

Secretary's report

Financial report

Election of committee and branch officers: Representative, Secretary, Treasurer

Talk by Guest speaker

Discussion on branch development, recruitment, organisation, administration

Motions

Date of next AGM

THERE WILL BE A BUFFET AND REFRESHMENTS AT THE CLOSE OF THE MEETING

Template for writing notes during a meeting

<table>
<tr><td>Date:
Time:
Place:</td><td colspan="2">Present:</td><td colspan="2">Apologies for absence:</td></tr>
<tr><td colspan="2">Discussion at the meeting</td><td colspan="3">Required follow-up after the meeting</td></tr>
<tr><td>Agenda item</td><td>Discussion</td><td>Action (WHAT)</td><td>Person responsible (WHO)</td><td>Timeframe / Deadline (WHEN)</td></tr>
<tr><td>1. Matters arising:</td><td></td><td></td><td></td><td></td></tr>
<tr><td>2.</td><td></td><td></td><td></td><td></td></tr>
<tr><td>3.</td><td></td><td></td><td></td><td></td></tr>
<tr><td>4.</td><td></td><td></td><td></td><td></td></tr>
<tr><td>5. AOB:</td><td></td><td></td><td></td><td></td></tr>
<tr><td colspan="5">Next Meeting
Date:
Time:
Place:</td></tr>
</table>

Sample notes written during a meeting

Date: *27 June* Time: *13.30* Place: *Boardroom*	Present: *DG, LB, PL, FG, YS, NM, CW, NB, JC, MS*		Apologies for absence: *JP*	
Discussion at the meeting		**Required follow-up after the meeting**		
Agenda item	Discussion	Action (WHAT)	Person responsible (WHO)	Timeframe / Deadline (WHEN)
1. Matters arising:	*All actions from minutes of quarterly meeting on 28 March completed. Minutes of quarterly meeting on 28 March were*			
2. *Directors' bonuses*	*New basis for calculation was approved.* *Payment schedule to be presented at next meeting*	*Circulate spreadsheet to Directors.* *Three alternative models to be defined*	*PL* *FG*	*by 1 July* *by 1 August*
3. *IT infrastructure*	*Medium-term plans were discussed.* *Investment options were outlined.* *Possible timescales were discussed.*	*Two plans to be circulated to Directors.* *Bank to be approached re funding.*	*NB* *CW*	*by 15 July* *by 1 September*
4. *Training, staff development and career development*	*Report findings were presented.* *Reasons for demotivation and dissatisfaction were reviewed .*	*Establish working group to provide concrete provisions for report recommendations 1, 3 and 6*	*DG to lead working group*	*by 15 August*
5. AOB:	*Environmental initiatives:* *MS presented ideas for sustainability. To be added to next agenda.*			

Next Meeting
Date: *September; date to be decided*
Time: *To be decided*
Place: *Boardroom?*

Minutes written using notes from previous page

Minutes of quarterly meeting held on 27 June 2011

Present: DG, LB, PL, FG, YS, NM, CW, NB, JC, MS
Apologies: JP

1. Matters arising

All actions from minutes of quarterly meeting on 28 March completed.

Minutes of quarterly meeting on 28 March were approved.

2. Directors' bonuses

1. A new basis for calculation was approved.
2. The payment schedule is to be presented at the next meeting.

The meeting agreed that:

1. PL will circulate spreadsheet to Directors by 1 July.
2. FG will define three alternative models by 1 August.

3. IT infrastructure

1. Medium-term plans were discussed.
2. Investment options were outlined.
3. Possible timescales were discussed.

The meeting agreed that:

1. NB will circulate two plans to the Directors by 15 July.
2. CW to approach a bank about funding by 1 September.
3. No decision has been made at this stage.

4. Training, staff development and career development

1. Report findings were presented.
2. Reasons for demotivation and dissatisfaction were reviewed.

The meeting agreed that:

1. DG would lead a working group with the aim of providing concrete provision for the report recommendations 1, 3 and 6. The working group should be held by 15 August.

5. AOB: Environmental initiatives

1. MS presented ideas for sustainability.
2. This matter should be added to the next agenda.

GLOSSARY

The most difficult words from each unit are defined here in this glossary. The definitions are extracts from the Collins COBUILD Advanced Dictionary.

Unit 1

con|cise ADJ Something that is **concise** says everything that is necessary without using any unnecessary words. • *Burton's text is concise and informative.* • *Whatever you are writing make sure you are clear, concise, and accurate.* • **con|cise|ly** ADV • *He'd delivered his report clearly and concisely.*

pre|cise ADJ Something that is **precise** is exact and accurate in all its details. • *They speak very precise English.* • *He does not talk too much and what he has to say is precise and to the point.*

ap|pro|pri|ate ADJ Something that is **appropriate** is suitable or acceptable for a particular situation. • *It is appropriate that Irish names dominate the list.* • *Dress neatly and attractively in an outfit appropriate to the job.* • *The teacher can then take appropriate action.* • **ap|pro|pri|ate|ly** ADV • *Dress appropriately and ask intelligent questions.* • *It's entitled, appropriately enough, 'Art for the Nation'.* • **ap|pro|pri|ate|ness** N-UNCOUNT • *He wonders about the appropriateness of each move he makes.*

ex|per|tise N-UNCOUNT **Expertise** is special skill or knowledge that is acquired by training, study, or practice. • *The problem is that most local authorities lack the expertise to deal sensibly in this market.*

re|dun|dant ADJ Something that is **redundant** is no longer needed because its job is being done by something else or because its job is no longer necessary or useful. • *Changes in technology may mean that once-valued skills are now redundant.* • *... the conversion of redundant buildings to residential use.*

ex|plic|it ADJ Something that is **explicit** is expressed or shown clearly and openly, without any attempt to hide anything. • *...explicit references to age in recruitment advertising.*

im|plic|it ADJ Something that is **implicit** is expressed in an indirect way. • *This is seen as an implicit warning not to continue with military action.*

Unit 2

pitch (pitches, pitching, pitched) VERB If something **is pitched at** a particular level or degree of difficulty, it is set at that level. • *I think the material is pitched at too high a level for our purposes.* • *The government has pitched High Street interest rates at a new level.*

ab|stract ADJ An **abstract** idea or way of thinking is based on general ideas rather than on real things and events. • *...abstract principles such as justice.* • *It's not a question of some abstract concept.* • *...the faculty of abstract reasoning.*

short cut (short cuts) also **short-cut** also **shortcut** N-COUNT A **short cut** is a quicker way of getting somewhere than the usual route. • *I tried to take a short cut and got lost.*

jar|gon N-UNCOUNT You use **jargon** to refer to words and expressions that are used in special or technical ways by particular groups of people, often making the language difficult to understand. • *The manual is full of the jargon and slang of self-improvement courses.* • *...the reading habits of 600,000 C2 males (marketing jargon for skilled manual workers).*

com|plex ADJ In grammar, a **complex** sentence contains one or more subordinate clauses as well as a main clause.

edit (edits, editing, edited) VERB If you **edit** a text such as an article or a book, you correct and adapt it so that it is suitable for publishing. • *The majority of contracts give the publisher the right to edit a book after it's done.* • *...an edited version of the speech.*

com|pe|tence N-UNCOUNT **Competence** is the ability to do something well or effectively. • *His competence as an economist had been reinforced by his successful fight against inflation.* • *We've always regarded him as a man of integrity and high professional competence.*

Unit 3

draft (drafts, drafting, drafted) VERB When you **draft** a letter, book, or speech, you write the first version of it. • *He drafted a standard letter to the editors.* • *The legislation was drafted by House Democrats.*

arouse (arouses, arousing, aroused) VERB If something **arouses** a particular feeling or instinct that exists in someone, it causes them to experience that feeling or instinct strongly. • *There is nothing like a long walk to arouse the appetite.* • *He aroused her mothering instincts.*

ex|tend (extends, extending, extended) VERB If you **extend** something, you make it longer or bigger. • *This year they have introduced three new products to extend their range.* • *The building was extended in 1500.* • *...an extended exhaust pipe.*

im|pact (impacts) N-COUNT The **impact** that something has **on** a situation, process, or person is a sudden and powerful effect that it has on them. • *They say they expect the meeting to have a marked impact on the future of the country.* • *The major impact of this epidemic worldwide is yet to come.* • *When an executive comes into a new job, he wants to quickly make an impact.*

im|petu|ous ADJ If you describe someone as **impetuous**, you mean that they are likely to act quickly and suddenly without thinking or being careful. • *He was young and impetuous.* • *He tended to react in a heated and impetuous way.*

re|mote (remoter, remotest) ADJ If you describe someone as **remote**, you mean that they behave as if they do not want to be friendly or closely involved with other people. • *She looked so beautiful, and at the same time so remote.* • **re|mote|ness** N-UNCOUNT • *His remoteness was resented.*

Unit 4

ac|knowl|edge|ment (acknowledgements) also **acknowledgment** N-COUNT An **acknowledgement** is a letter or message that you receive from someone, telling you that something you have sent to them has arrived. • *I have received neither an acknowledgment nor a reply.*

dif|fer|en|ti|ate (differentiates, differentiating, differentiated) VERB If you **differentiate between** things or if you **differentiate** one thing **from** another, you recognize or show the difference between them. • *A child may not differentiate between his imagination and the real world.* • *At this age your baby cannot differentiate one person from another.*

emer|gence N-UNCOUNT The **emergence of** something is the process or event of its coming into existence. • *...the emergence of new democracies in East and Central Europe.*

blend (blends, blending, blended) VERB If you **blend** ideas, policies, or styles, you use them together in order to achieve something. • *His 'cosmic vision' is to blend Christianity with 'the wisdom of all world religions'.* • *...a band that blended jazz, folk and classical music.*

en|coun|ter (encounters) N-COUNT An **encounter with** someone is a meeting with them, particularly one that is unexpected or significant. • *The author tells of a remarkable encounter with a group of South Vietnamese soldiers.*

chat|ty ADJ A **chatty** style of writing or talking is friendly and informal. • *He wrote a chatty letter to his wife.*

Unit 5

in|cen|tive (incentives) N-VAR If something is an **incentive to** do something, it encourages you to do it. • *There is little or no incentive to adopt such measures.* • *Many companies in Britain are keen on the idea of tax incentives for R&D.*

oc|cur|rence (occurrences) N-COUNT An **occurrence** is something that happens. *(formal)* • *Complaints seemed to be an everyday occurrence.* • *The food queues have become a daily occurrence across the country.*

de|duc|tive ADJ **Deductive** reasoning involves drawing conclusions logically from other things that are already known. *(formal)* • *She didn't seem at all impressed by his deductive powers.*

in|duc|tive ADJ **Inductive** reasoning is based on the process of induction.

chrono|logi|cal ADJ If things are described or shown in **chronological** order, they are described or shown in the order in which they happened. • *I have arranged these stories in chronological order.* • **chrono|logi|cal|ly** ADV • *The exhibition is organised chronologically.*

rig|id ADJ Laws, rules, or systems that are **rigid** cannot be changed or varied, and are therefore considered to be rather severe. • *Several colleges in our study have rigid rules about student conduct.* • *Hospital routines for nurses are very rigid.*

Unit 6

em|phat|ic ADJ An **emphatic** response or statement is one made in a forceful way, because the speaker feels very strongly about what they are saying. • *His response was immediate and emphatic.* • *I answered both questions with an emphatic 'Yes'.*

en|gag|ing ADJ An **engaging** person or thing is pleasant, interesting, and entertaining. • *...one of her most engaging and least known novels.* • *He was engaging company.*

or|gan|ic ADJ **Organic** change or development happens gradually and naturally rather than suddenly. *(formal)* • *...to manage the company and supervise its organic growth.*

mile|stone (milestones) N-COUNT A **milestone** is an important event in the history or development of something or someone. • *He said the launch of the party represented a milestone in Zambian history.* • *Starting school is a milestone for both children and parents.*

re|sili|ent ADJ People and things that are **resilient** are able to recover easily and quickly from unpleasant or damaging events. • *George Fraser was clearly a good soldier, calm and resilient.* • *When the U.S. stock market collapsed in October 1987, the Japanese stock market was the most resilient.* • **re|sili|ence** N-UNCOUNT • *... the resilience of human beings to fight after they've been attacked.*

Unit 7

col|labo|ra|tive ADJ A **collaborative** piece of work is done by two or more people or groups working together. *(formal)* • *...a collaborative research project.* • *'The First Day' is their first collaborative album.* • **col|labo|ra|tive|ly** ADV • *He was not the kind of artist who worked collaboratively.*

clar|ity N-UNCOUNT The **clarity** of something such as a book or argument is its quality of being well explained and easy to understand. • *...the ease and clarity with which the author explains difficult technical and scientific subjects.*

vague (vaguer, vaguest) ADJ If something written or spoken is **vague**, it does not explain or express things clearly. • *A lot of the talk was apparently vague and general.* • *The description was pretty vague.* • *...vague information.*

as|ser|tive ADJ Someone who is **assertive** states their needs and opinions clearly, so that people take notice. • *Women have become more assertive in the past decade.* • *...an assertive style of management.*

har|mo|ny N-UNCOUNT If people are living **in harmony with** each other, they are living together peacefully rather than fighting or arguing. • *We must try to live in peace and harmony with ourselves and those around us.* • *He projected himself as the protector of national unity and harmony.*

ori|ent|ed or **orientated** ADJ If someone **is oriented towards** or **oriented to** a particular thing or person, they are mainly concerned with that thing or person. • *It seems almost inevitable that North African economies will still be primarily oriented towards Europe.* • *Most students here are oriented to computers.*

over|haul (overhauls, overhauling, overhauled) VERB If you **overhaul** a system or method, you examine it carefully and make many changes in it in order to improve it. • *The government said it wanted to overhaul the employment training scheme to make it cost effective.* • *The legal system needs to be overhauled.* N-COUNT • **Overhaul** is also a noun. • *The study says there must be a complete overhaul of air traffic control systems.*

Unit 8

di|rect ADJ If you describe a person or their behaviour as **direct**, you mean that they are honest and open, and say exactly what they mean. • *He avoided giving a direct answer.* • *The new songs are more direct.* • *No direct reference was made to the call by the Foreign Office minister.* • **di|rect|ness** N-UNCOUNT • *Using 'I' adds directness to a piece of writing.* • *'I like Rupert enormously,' she said, with a directness which made Pat flush.*

omit (omits, omitting, omitted) VERB If you **omit to** do something, you do not do it. *(formal)* • *His new girlfriend had omitted to tell him she was married.*

neu|tral ADJ If someone speaks in a **neutral** voice or if the expression on their face is **neutral**, they do not show what they are thinking or feeling. • *Isabel put her magazine down and said in a neutral voice, 'You're very late, darling.'* • *He told her about the death, describing the events in as neutral a manner as he could.*

ut|most ADJ You can use **utmost** to emphasize the importance or seriousness of something or to emphasize the way that it is done. • *It is a matter of the utmost urgency to find out what has happened to these people.* • *Security matters are treated with the utmost seriousness.* • *You should proceed with the utmost caution.* • *Utmost care must be taken not to spill any of the contents.*

re|gret (regrets, regretting, regretted) VERB You can say that you **regret** something as a polite way of saying that you are sorry about it. You use expressions such as **I regret to say** or **I regret to inform you** to show that you are sorry about something. • *'I very much regret the injuries he sustained,' he said.* • *I regret that the United States has added its voice to such protests.* • *Her lack of co-operation is nothing new, I regret to say.* • *I regret to inform you he died as a consequence of his injuries.*

budg|et|ary ADJ A **budgetary** matter or policy is concerned with the amount of money that is available to a country or organization, and how it is to be spent. *(formal)* • *There are huge budgetary pressures on all governments in Europe to reduce their armed forces.*

Unit 9

straight|forward ADJ If you describe a person or their behaviour as **straightforward**, you approve of them because they are honest and direct, and do not try to hide their feelings. • *She is very blunt, very straightforward and very honest.* • *I was impressed by his straightforward intelligent manner.* • **straight|forward|ly** • *His daughter says straightforwardly that he was not good enough.*

lay|er (layers) N-COUNT If something such as a system or an idea has many **layers**, it has many different levels or parts. • *...an astounding ten layers of staff between the factory worker and the chief executive.* • *Critics and the public puzzle out the layers of meaning in his photos.*

jus|ti|fi|ca|tion (justifications) N-VAR A **justification for** something is an acceptable reason or explanation for it. • *To me the only justification for a zoo is educational.* • *I knew from the beginning that there was no justification for what I was doing.*

neg|li|gent ADJ If someone in a position of responsibility is **negligent**, they do not do something which they ought to do. • *The jury determined that the airline was negligent in training and supervising the crew.* • *The Council had acted in a negligent manner.* • **neg|li|gent|ly** ADV • *A manufacturer negligently made and marketed a car with defective brakes.*

fit|ting ADJ Something that is **fitting** is right or suitable. • *A solitary man, it was perhaps fitting that he should have died alone.* • *The President's address was a fitting end to a bitter campaign.* • **fit|ting|ly** ADV • *...the four-storeyed, and fittingly named, High House.* • *Fittingly, she will spend her year off training her voice to sing blues and jazz.*

sole ADJ The **sole** thing or person of a particular type is the only one of that type. • *Their sole aim is to destabilize the Indian government.*

Unit 10

over|come (overcomes, overcoming, overcame)

> The form **overcome** is used in the present tense and is also the past participle.

VERB If you **overcome** a problem or a feeling, you successfully deal with it and control it. • *Molly had fought and overcome her fear of flying.* • *Find a way to overcome your difficulties.*

ex|pres|sion (expressions) N-COUNT An **expression** is a word or phrase. • *She spoke in a quiet voice but used remarkably coarse expressions.*

evolve (evolves, evolving, evolved) VERB If something **evolves** or you **evolve** it, it gradually develops over a period of time into something different and usually more advanced. • *...a tiny airline which eventually evolved into Pakistan International Airlines.* • *Popular music evolved from folk songs.* • *As medical knowledge evolves, beliefs change.* • *This was when he evolved the working method from which he has never departed.*

sub|sti|tute (substitutes) N-COUNT A **substitute** is something that you have or use instead of something else. • *She is seeking a substitute for the very man whose departure made her cry.* • *...tests on humans to find a blood substitute made from animal blood.*

inter|act (interacts, interacting, interacted) VERB When people **interact with** each other or **interact**, they communicate as they work or spend time together. • *While the other children interacted and played together, Ted ignored them.* • *...rhymes and songs to help parents interact with their babies.* • **inter|ac|tion** (interactions) N-VAR • *This can sometimes lead to somewhat superficial interactions with other people.* • *...our experience of informal social interaction among adults.*

ob|serv|able ADJ Something that is **observable** can be seen. • *Mars is too faint and too low in the sky to be observable.*

Unit 11

clari|fy (clarifies, clarifying, clarified) VERB To **clarify** something means to make it easier to understand, usually by explaining it in more detail. *(formal)* • *Thank you for writing and allowing me to clarify the present position.* • *A bank spokesman was unable to clarify the situation.* • **clari|fi|ca|tion** (clarifications) N-VAR • *The union has written to Zurich asking for clarification of the situation.*

ap|prov|al N-UNCOUNT If you win someone's **approval for** something that you ask for or suggest, they agree to it. • *...efforts to win congressional approval for an aid package for Moscow.* • *The chairman has also given his approval for an investigation into the case.* • *The proposed modifications met with widespread approval.*

as|sur|ance (assurances) N-VAR If you give someone an **assurance that** something is true or will happen, you say that it is definitely true or will definitely happen, in order to make them feel less worried. • *He would like an assurance that other forces will not move into the territory that his forces vacate.* • *He will have been pleased by Marshal Yazov's assurance of the armed forces' loyalty.*

ac|claim (acclaims, acclaiming, acclaimed) VERB If someone or something **is acclaimed**, they are praised enthusiastically. *(formal)* • *She has been acclaimed for the TV drama 'Prime Suspect'.* • *He was acclaimed as England's greatest modern painter.* • *The group's debut album was immediately acclaimed a hip hop classic.* • **ac|claimed** ADJ • *She has published six highly acclaimed novels.*

over|all ADJ You use **overall** to indicate that you are talking about a situation in general or about the whole of something. • *...the overall rise in unemployment.* • *Cut down your overall amount of physical activity.* • *It is usually the woman who assumes overall care of the baby.* ADV • **Overall** is also an adverb. • *Overall, I like Connie. I think she's great.* • *Overall I was disappointed.* • *The college has few ways to assess the quality of education overall.*

ur|gent ADJ If something is **urgent**, it needs to be dealt with as soon as possible. • *There is an urgent need for food and water.* • *He had urgent business in New York.* • **ur|gen|cy** N-UNCOUNT • *The urgency of finding a cure attracted some of the best minds in medical science.* • *It is a matter of utmost urgency.*

li|aise (liaises, liaising, liaised) VERB When organizations or people **liaise**, or when one organization **liaises with** another, they work together and keep each other informed about what is happening. • *Detectives are liaising with Derbyshire police following the bomb explosion early today.* • *The three groups will all liaise with each other to help the child.* • *Social services and health workers liaise closely.*

Unit 12

temp|ta|tion **(temptations)** N-VAR If you feel you want to do something or have something, even though you know you really should avoid it, you can refer to this feeling as **temptation**. You can also refer to the thing you want to do or have as a **temptation**. • *Will they be able to resist the temptation to buy?* • *...the many temptations to which you will be exposed.*

tran|si|tion **(transitions)** N-VAR **Transition** is the process in which something changes from one state to another. • *The transition to a multi-party democracy is proving to be difficult.* • *...a period of transition.*

ab|rupt ADJ Someone who is **abrupt** speaks in a rather rude, unfriendly way. • *He was abrupt to the point of rudeness.* • *Cross was a little taken aback by her abrupt manner.* • **ab|rupt|ly** ADV • *'Good night, then,' she said abruptly.* • **ab|rupt|ness** N-UNCOUNT • *I think Simon was hurt by your abruptness this afternoon.*

round off PHRASAL VERB If you **round off** an activity with something, you end the activity by doing something that provides a clear or satisfactory conclusion to it. • *The Italian way is to round off a meal with an ice-cream.* • *...a dazzling firework display which rounded off a lovely day.* • *This rounded the afternoon off perfectly.* • *He rounds off by proposing a toast to the attendants.*

prompt ADJ A **prompt** action is done without any delay. • *It is not too late, but prompt action is needed.* • *...an inflammation of the eyeball which needs prompt treatment.*

ful|fil|ment also **fulfillment** N-UNCOUNT **The fulfilment of** a promise, threat, request, hope, or duty is the event or act of it happening or being made to happen. • *Visiting Angkor was the fulfilment of a childhood dream.*

time frame **(time frames)** N-COUNT The **time frame** of an event is the length of time during which it happens or develops. *(formal)* • *The time frame within which all this occurred was from September 1985 to March 1986.* • *Discussions at the U.N. could include a time frame for action.*

Unit 13

den|sity **(densities)** N-VAR **Density** is the extent to which something is filled or covered with people or things. • *...a law which restricts the density of housing.* • *The region has a very high population density.* • *...areas with high densities of immigrant populations.*

im|press **(impresses, impressing, impressed)** VERB If something **impresses** you, you feel great admiration for it. • *What impressed him most was their speed.* • *...a group of students who were trying to impress their girlfriends.* • *Cannon's film impresses on many levels.* • **im|pressed** ADJ • *I was very impressed by one young man at my lectures.* • *I'm very impressed with the new airport.* • *He went away suitably impressed.*

frag|ment **(fragments, fragmenting, fragmented)** VERB If something **fragments** or **is fragmented**, it breaks or separates into small pieces or parts. • *The clouds fragmented and out came the sun.* • *Fierce rivalries have traditionally fragmented the region.* • *By the first century BC, Buddhism was in danger of fragmenting into small sects.*

sus|tain|able ADJ You use **sustainable** to describe the use of natural resources when this use is kept at a steady level that is not likely to damage the environment. • *...the management, conservation and sustainable development of forests.* • *Try to buy wood that you know has come from a sustainable source.* • **sus|tain|abil|ity** N-UNCOUNT • *...the growing concern about environmental sustainability.* • **sus|tain|ably** ADV • *It wants timber to come, where possible, from sustainably managed sources.*

mis|sion N-SING If you say that you have a **mission**, you mean that you have a strong commitment and sense of duty to do or achieve something. • *He viewed his mission in life as protecting the weak from the evil.* • *There is an enormous sense of mission in his speech and gesture.*

con|sti|tute **(constitutes, constituting, constituted)** V-LINK If something **constitutes** a particular thing, it can be regarded as being that thing. • *Testing patients without their consent would constitute a professional and legal offence.* • *The vote hardly constitutes a victory.* • *What constitutes abuse?*

under|ly|ing ADJ The **underlying** features of an object, event, or situation are not obvious, and it may be difficult to discover or reveal them. • *To stop a problem you have to understand its underlying causes.* • *I think that the underlying problem is education, unemployment and bad housing.*

Unit 14

skim **(skims, skimming, skimmed)** VERB If you **skim** a piece of writing, you read through it quickly. • *He skimmed the pages quickly, then read them again more carefully.* • *I only had time to skim through the script before I flew over here.*

la|bel (labels, labelling, labelled)

in AM, use **labeling**, **labeled**

VERB If something **is labelled**, a label is attached to it giving information about it. • *The stuff has never been properly logged and labelled.* • *Meat labelled 'Scotch Beef' sells for a premium in supermarkets.* • *All the products are labelled with comprehensive instructions.*

scan (scans, scanning, scanned) VERB When you **scan** written material, you look through it quickly in order to find important or interesting information. • *She scanned the advertisement pages of the newspapers.* • *I haven't read much into it as yet. I've only just scanned through it.* N-SING • **Scan** is also a noun. • *I just had a quick scan through your book again.*

se|quence (sequences) N-COUNT A particular **sequence** is a particular order in which things happen or are arranged. • *...the colour sequence yellow, orange, purple, blue, green and white.* • *The chronological sequence gives the book an element of structure.*

am|bi|gu|ity (ambiguities) N-VAR If you say that there is **ambiguity** in something, you mean that it is unclear or confusing, or it can be understood in more than one way. • *There is considerable ambiguity about what this part of the agreement actually means.* • *...the ambiguities of language.*

Unit 15

stream|line (streamlines, streamlining, streamlined) VERB To **streamline** an organization or process means to make it more efficient by removing unnecessary parts of it. • *They're making efforts to streamline their normally cumbersome bureaucracy.* • *They say things should be better now that they have streamlined application procedures.*

stick to If you **stick to** rules, you do what they say you must do. • *Obviously we are disappointed but the committee could do nothing less than stick to the rules.* • *Police must stick to the highest standards if they are to win back public confidence.*

time-consuming also **time consuming** ADJ If something is **time-consuming**, it takes a lot of time. • *It's just very time consuming to get such a large quantity of data.* • *Starting a new business, however small, is a time-consuming exercise.*

give and take PHRASE If you say that something requires **give and take**, you mean that people must compromise or co-operate for it to be successful. • *...a happy relationship where there's a lot of give and take.*

gain (gains, gaining, gained) VERB If you **gain from** something such as an event or situation, you get some advantage or benefit from it. • *The company didn't disclose how much it expects to gain from the two deals.* • *There is absolutely nothing to be gained by feeling bitter.* • *It is sad that a major company should try to gain from other people's suffering.*

draft (drafts, drafting, drafted) N-COUNT A **draft** is an early version of a letter, book, or speech. • *I rewrote his rough draft, which was published under my name.* • *I faxed a first draft of this article to him.* • *...a draft report from a major U.S. university.* • *...a draft law.*

firm (firmer, firmest) ADJ If you describe someone as **firm**, you mean they behave in a way that shows that they are not going to change their mind, or that they are the person who is in control. • *She had to be firm with him. 'I don't want to see you again.'* • *Perhaps they need the guiding hand of a firm father figure.*

Unit 16

proof|read (proofreads, proofreading) also **proof-read** VERB When someone **proofreads** something such as a book or an article, they read it before it is published in order to find and mark mistakes that need to be corrected. • *I didn't even have the chance to proofread my own report.*

ac|cu|ra|cy N-UNCOUNT The **accuracy of** information or measurements is their quality of being true or correct, even in small details. • *We cannot guarantee the accuracy of these figures.*

over|load (overloads, overloading, overloaded) VERB To **overload** someone **with** work, problems, or information means to give them more work, problems, or information than they can cope with. • *...an effective method that will not overload staff with yet more paperwork.* N-UNCOUNT • **Overload** is also a noun. • *57 per cent complained of work overload.* • *The greatest danger is that we simply create information overload for our executives.*

thor|ough • **thor|ough|ly** ADV • *Food that is being offered hot must be reheated thoroughly.* • *...a thoroughly researched and illuminating biography.* • **thor|ough|ly** ADV • *I thoroughly enjoy your programme.* • *We returned home thoroughly contented.*

lin|ear ADJ A **linear** process or development is one in which something changes or progresses straight from one stage to another, and has a starting point and an ending point. • *Her novel subverts the conventions of linear narrative. It has no neat chronology and no tidy denouement.* • *...the linear view of time, with the idea that the past is moving into the present and the present into the future.*

trust (trusts, trusting, trusted) VERB If you **trust** someone, you believe that they are honest and sincere and will not deliberately do anything to harm you. • *'I trust you completely,' he said.* • *He did argue in a general way that the president can't be trusted.* • **trust|ed** ADJ • *After speaking to a group of her most trusted advisers, she turned her anger into action.*

post|pone (postpones, postponing, postponed) VERB If you **postpone** an event, you delay it or arrange for it to take place at a later time than was originally planned. • *He decided to postpone the expedition until the following day.* • *The visit has now been postponed indefinitely.*

Unit 17

sum|mary (summaries) N-COUNT A **summary of** something is a short account of it, which gives the main points but not the details. • *What follows is a brief summary of the process.* • *Here's a summary of the day's news.* • *Milligan gives a fair summary of his subject within a relatively short space.* PHRASE You use **in summary** to indicate that what you are about to say is a summary of what has just been said. • *In summary, it is my opinion that this complete treatment process was very successful.*

con|clu|sion (conclusions) N-COUNT When you come to a **conclusion**, you decide that something is true after you have thought about it carefully and have considered all the relevant facts. • *Over the years I've come to the conclusion that she's a very great musician.* • *I have tried to give some idea of how I feel–other people will no doubt draw their own conclusions.*

pie chart (pie charts) N-COUNT A **pie chart** is a circle divided into sections to show the relative proportions of a set of things.

bar chart (bar charts) N-COUNT A **bar chart** is a graph which uses parallel rectangular shapes to represent changes in the size, value, or rate of something or to compare the amount of something relating to a number of different countries or groups. *(mainly brit)* • *The bar chart below shows the huge growth of U.K. car exports over the past few years.*

in AM, use **bar graph**

ra|tion|al ADJ **Rational** decisions and thoughts are based on reason rather than on emotion. • *He's asking you to look at both sides of the case and come to a rational decision.* • *Mary was able to short-circuit her stress response by keeping her thoughts calm and rational.*

com|mon|al|ity (commonalities) N-VAR **Commonality** is used to refer to a feature or purpose that is shared by two or more people or things. *(formal)* • *We don't have the same commonality of interest.* • *There are an amazing number of commonalities between systems.*

Unit 18

agen|da (agendas) N-COUNT An **agenda** is a list of the items that have to be discussed at a meeting. • *This is sure to be an item on the agenda next week.* • *High on the agenda of tomorrow's meeting will be the turmoil in Japan.*

chair N-COUNT The person who is the **chair of** a committee or meeting is the person in charge of it. • *She is the chair of the Defense Advisory Committee on Women in the Military.*

prin|ci|pal (principals) ADJ **Principal** means first in order of importance. • *The principal reason for my change of mind is this.* • *...the country's principal source of foreign exchange earnings.* • *Their principal concern is bound to be that of winning the next general election.*

cir|cu|late (circulates, circulating, circulated) VERB If a piece of writing **circulates** or **is circulated**, copies of it are passed round among a group of people. • *The document was previously circulated in New York at the United Nations.* • *Public employees, teachers and liberals are circulating a petition for his recall.* • *This year anonymous leaflets have been circulating in Beijing.*

brev|ity N-UNCOUNT The **brevity of** something is the fact that it is short or lasts for only a short time. *(formal)* • *The bonus of this homely soup is the brevity of its cooking time.* • *The brevity of the letter concerned me.*

back up If someone or something **backs up** a statement, they supply evidence to suggest that it is true. • *Radio signals received from the galaxy's centre back up the black hole theory.* • *Her views are backed up by a 1989 Home Office report on crime.*

Unit 19

shift (shifts, shifting, shifted) VERB If you **shift** something or if it **shifts**, it moves slightly. • *He stopped, shifting his cane to his left hand.* • *He shifted from foot to foot.* • *The entire pile shifted and slid, thumping onto the floor.* • *...the squeak of his boots in the snow as he shifted his weight.*

blank (blanks, blanking, blanked) ADJ Something that is **blank** has nothing on it. • *We could put some of the pictures over on that blank wall over there.* • *He tore a blank page from his notebook.* • *...blank cassettes.*

scroll (scrolls, scrolling, scrolled) VERB If you **scroll** through text on a computer screen, you move the text up or down to find the information that you need. *(computing)* • *I scrolled down to find 'United States of America'.*

sprin|kle (sprinkles, sprinkling, sprinkled) VERB If something **is sprinkled with** particular things, it has a few of them throughout it and they are far apart from each other. • *Unfortunately, the text is sprinkled with errors.* • *Men in green army* *uniforms are sprinkled throughout the huge auditorium.*

dis|claim|er (disclaimers) N-COUNT A **disclaimer** is a statement in which a person says that they did not know about something or that they are not responsible for something. *(formal)* • *The disclaimer asserts that the company won't be held responsible for any inaccuracies.*

stand|ard|ize (standardizes, standardizing, standardized)

in BRIT, also use **standardise**

VERB To **standardize** things means to change them so that they all have the same features. • *There is a drive both to standardise components and to reduce the number of models on offer.* • *He feels standardized education does not benefit those children who are either below or above average intelligence.* • **stand|ardi|za|tion** N-UNCOUNT • *...the standardisation of working hours in Community countries.*

ad|ap|ta|tion (adaptations) N-UNCOUNT **Adaptation** is the act of changing something or changing your behaviour to make it suitable for a new purpose or situation. • *Most living creatures are capable of adaptation when compelled to do so.*

Unit 20

strength (strengths) N-VAR Someone's **strengths** are the qualities and abilities that they have which are an advantage to them, or which make them successful. • *Take into account your own strengths and weaknesses.* • *Vision and ambition are his great strengths.* • *Tact was never Mr Moore's strength.* • *Organisation is the strength of any good army.* • *The book's strength lay in its depiction of present-day Tokyo.*

weak (weaker, weakest) ADJ Your **weak** points are the qualities or talents you do not possess, or the things you are not very good at. • *You may very well be asked what your weak points are. Don't try to claim you don't have any.* • *Geography was my weak subject.* • *His short stories tend to be weak on plot.* • **weak|ness** N-VAR • *His only weakness is his temperament.* • *There's some weakness in their teaching ability.*

weak|ness (weaknesses) N-COUNT If you have a **weakness for** something, you like it very much, although this is perhaps surprising or undesirable. • *Stephen himself had a weakness for cats.* • *His one weakness, apart from aeroplanes, is ice cream.*

suc|cess (successes) N-UNCOUNT **Success** is the achievement of something that you have been trying to do. • *It's important for the long-term success of any diet that you vary your meals.* • *...the success of European business in building a stronger partnership between management and workers.*

down|play (downplays, downplaying, downplayed) VERB If you **downplay** a fact or feature, you try to make people think that it is less important or serious than it really is. • *The government is trying to downplay the violence.* • *...to downplay the dangers of nuclear accidents.*

vir|tu|ous ADJ If you describe someone as **virtuous**, you mean that they have done what they ought to do and feel very pleased with themselves, perhaps too pleased. • *I cleaned the flat, which left me feeling virtuous.* • **vir|tu|ous|ly** ADV • *'I've already done that,' said Ronnie virtuously.*

pat (pats, patting, patted) If you give someone **a pat on the back** or if you **pat** them **on the back**, you show them that you think they have done well and deserve to be praised. • *The players deserve a pat on the back.* • *If you do something well, give yourself a pat on the back.*

ANSWER KEY

UNIT 1

1

1 (advance) planning
2 (advance) reservations
3 all meet (together)
4 (basic) fundamentals
5 cheap (price)
6 (close) proximity
7 (difficult) challenge
8 (each and) every OR each (and every)
9 (end) result
10 estimated (roughly) at
11 (general) public
12 (past) experience
13 reason is (because)
14 (regular) routine
15 (unexpected) surprise

2

Dear customer

We have received your request to return the faulty monitor, ~~which is not displaying the correct colours~~. We will process this as fast as possible. In order to provide a quick and reliable service, we kindly ask you to follow these instructions closely:

Within the next twelve hours, you will receive two e-mails from GTS. In the first e-mail you will find a link to a GTS return label. Please print out this label with a laser printer. ********************. With this number you can track the delivery status of your item on the internet.

Please pack your defective device into its original packaging. Afterwards please clearly stick the return label on the box ~~so that it is easily visible~~. When your parcel is ready for collection, please call GTS to arrange for collection. ********************

Make sure you pack your defective device in the original packaging. If you don't have the original packaging or any other secure packaging for transportation, contact us by email so that we can provide you with suitable packaging. ~~Please let us know~~.

Please only send in your defective LCD display together with its stand and the external power adapter (without its power cord). You will be charged for extra shipping costs in case we need to send back any accessories which you sent to us in error.

Yours sincerely

Electronic Computer Services

3

a The content is:

- too detailed, as the information repeats what the reader can expect to find in the CV
- missing information about personality and soft skills

b The content is:

- too brief
- too vague

4

a Suggested content:

- Give a general overview of your suitability
- Point out your specific experience in relation to the position
- Give information about awards and special responsibilities
- Include information about your personality and soft skills

Model email

Dear Mr Smith

I am responding to your advertisement in *The Daily Observer* of 8 January 2011, regarding the Automotive Sales Representative position. Attached is my CV, showing my education, experience, and background.

(Give a general overview of your suitability)
As you will see from my CV, I gained a degree in Business Administration. During my final year I specialised in sales and marketing, areas that I became particularly interested in. After graduation,

I decided to follow a career in sales and marketing. You will find more details in my CV.

(Point out your specific experience in relation to the position)
In relation to the specific requirements listed in the advertisement, I have five years' experience in the sales and marketing field. From this I developed skills in planning and advertising, organising events, distribution, and sponsorship. In addition, I have experience of working within the motor industry, as a sales executive at the Q Cars dealership network.

(Give information about awards and special responsibilities)
Throughout my sales and marketing career I have won top sales awards, and, in my last job, was involved in training other sales representatives in specific sales techniques to increase their sales.

(Include information about your personality and soft skills).
I am regarded as an outgoing person who can talk to people at all levels and have been complimented on my ability both to communicate clearly with and listen to others. I have recognised that I also enjoy working with the public, demonstrating products, and educating others in their uses. I believe I would excel in automotive sales because I find sales a challenging and rewarding career.

I hope my application will be of interest to you.
I am available to come in for interview at a mutually convenient time. I look forward to hearing from you.

Yours sincerely

Mary Green

b Suggested content:

- Write why you want the internship
- Point out your specific experience in relation to the intern position
- Include awards and scholarships to show you are a suitable candidate

Model email

Dear Ms Bryant

I would like to apply for the scientific research internship that was advertised in the University Career Services Office.

(Write why you want the internship)
I believe that this position will help me gain the necessary experience to find a job as a laboratory researcher in the field of environmental risk analysis.

(Point out your specific experience in relation to the intern position)
The attached CV shows the details of my education and practical skills. In particular, I would like to point out that I have already gained laboratory experience in chemistry, biology, and geology, both indoors and in the field. In the lab, I have performed chemical reactions and I am currently using microscopes to observe many specimens. In environmental field studies, I have conducted outdoor experiments to assess water chemistry.

(Include awards and scholarships to show you are a suitable candidate)
During my final year at university, I gained a distinction for my practical work in soil investigation.

I hope my application will be of interest to you.
I am available to come in for interview at a mutually convenient time. I look forward to hearing from you.

Yours sincerely

Sarah Bentley

UNIT 2

1

Why is it difficult to understand?

- Too much technical detail
- Complex vocabulary
- Long sentences

Suggested improvement

During three years at XYZ and four years at ABC I built up a broad fundamental knowledge of food science and processing. As I wished to extend my activities through to product completion, I needed to be able to communicate with both the scientifically-focused, laboratory-based personnel and the process-driven pilot plant research groups. In the international working environments at XYZ and ABC, I gained the necessary interpersonal skills to reduce cultural and scientific misunderstandings. In addition, I used my language skills fully to achieve optimal project results and friendly working relationships.

2

Why is it difficult to understand?

- Long sentences
- Too much technical detail
- Too many abbreviations

Suggested improvement

This year we have reviewed our quality improvement plan in order to focus on and align with the new Blueprint For Excellence. As a result, we are working towards meeting future expectations. This will enable us to produce a document that is easier to use and adapt in the future. We expect that this will meet with the approval of the Business Growth Designers Forum (BGDF).

3

Why is it difficult to understand?

- Jargon

- **Suggested improvement**

Our new product has the following features:

- latest technology
- easy to use
- innovative
- robust
- flexible

It delivers high performance and can easily be adapted to client needs.

4

Why is it difficult to understand?

- Complexity of vocabulary
- Sentence length
- Sentence structure

Suggested improvement

If anything happens, it's not our fault.

UNIT 3

1

The four-box document plan

1. Recommend new system

Concern about selection of most suitable suppliers – price and quality

Recommend introduction of new evaluation system for suppliers

Replace existing system with more transparent system

Results: more transparency and savings

2. Why change?

Old system

- Based on local suppliers
- List main disadvantages

New system

- Use e-procurement
- List main advantages

3. Detailed information

Categories for supplier evaluation

Procedure for introduction

Changes to documentation

Training in use of new system

4. What next?

Directors to review new system

Discussion at next meeting

Decision on implementation within four weeks

Proposed timescale for implementation

2

Categories for supplier evaluation

3

Suggested key

1. Introduction

- Original report
- Current proposal

2. Benefits of home-working

- Improvement in customer service
- Savings in accommodation (space and cost)
- Positive implications for recruitment and retention of staff
- Opportunity to balance work with other aspects of their life, in particular care responsibilities
- Opportunity for individuals previously unable to enter or remain in work
- Fewer office interruptions results in increased productivity

3. Challenges of home-working

- Stay focused on the job; avoid distractions
- Stick to designated hours
- Set up a work phone number and email address; only give details out to clients and potential customers
- Turn off personal mobile phone and let the home phone go to the answering machine
- Plan work and social life separately

4. Conclusions and next steps

Home-working can:

- Increase efficiency and cost savings
- Maintain and even improve performance
- 'Cost benefit analysis report' attached
- Further detailed discussions will be needed before offering home-working to new groups of employees
- Group consultation with department heads 4 September 2011
- Before meeting, department heads to familiarise selves with attached documentation

UNIT 4

1

Dear Nick

Many thanks for getting back to me so promptly. It's great to hear that you are interested in working with us. Apologies for my delay in replying. I was unwell last week.

With regards to timing and details, we plan to have the main tasks for this project ready by the middle of October. We would send you the task list then, and would like you to devise a number of categories with which to label certain key business categories. We would like to receive the list, arranged according to category, by the middle of November. Please could you let me know whether this would be acceptable to you.

We are still looking into your suggestion about the scope of the additional notes. At this stage, we have not made a final decision. I plan to discuss this with my team next week and aim to send you more details over the next two weeks.

Please could you let me know whether you would be interested in working on the main tasks, as outlined above. For the additional notes, I realise you don't have much information yet and may not be able to give us an answer.

I look forward to hearing from you.

With best wishes

Lisa

2

Dear Mr Bennett

There can be no denying that we are experiencing times of unprecedented economic uncertainty. As a new UK bank, Maximore believe it's vital that we really understand the issues that savers are confronted with today. Which is why I'm writing to invite you, as a valued Maximore Savings customer, to take part in our first Customer Survey.

Make your voice heard in just a few minutes
With a few simple questions and a few minutes of your time, we can begin to understand what matters to you. We want to increase awareness in the media of the challenges savers face. By sharing your feedback with selected financial journalists we hope to draw attention to the issues that really matter to you and maybe even start the wheels of change. We will of course also use your feedback to see how we can also help you to overcome some of the issues you currently experience as a saver.

Win £50 Harwells vouchers
As a thank you, on completing the survey you can enter our free prize draw to win one of twenty £50 Harwells gift vouchers.

Your opinion is important – join Maximore Customer Survey Panel
You will also have the opportunity to join our new Customer Survey Panel. Joining our Panel means you will exclusively be invited to take part in future surveys and have your say on other issues which affect you. And of course, you'll have the chance to win even more vouchers.

Completing the survey is simple and your answers are anonymous. Just click on the link and follow the instructions online. The survey is open until midnight Sunday 24 October 2011.

Thank you in advance for your time and feedback.

Kind regards

Annetta Sherbourne
Customer Relations Manager

3

Dear Mr Henley

Thank you for your recent claim for reimbursement of expenses, incurred as a result of the disruption to your flight from Rotaronga to London Heathrow. We wish to assure you that we did everything in our power to minimise the consequences for all passengers. Therefore we deeply regret that we were unable to assist you as much as we would have wished in this difficult situation. We apologise for any inconvenience you experienced as a result.

As the flight irregularities that occurred were clearly due to 'force majeure', we are only able to offer you limited financial compensation, based on:

- reasonable expenses incurred
- approved receipts provided
- costs directly linked to travel delays

Having assessed your claim, and as a gesture of goodwill we will credit an amount of GBP100 to your bank account. In order to make the transfer, could you please provide us with the following information:

- Account name:
- Bank name:
- Swift code:
- IBAN number:

We appreciate you taking the time to inform us about your experience and we hope that this incident will not discourage you and your family from choosing Rotarongan International Airlines in your future travel arrangements.

Yours sincerely

Maryam Mobara
Feedback Management
Rotarongan International Airlines Ltd.

UNIT 5

1

In short	In addition	too
Obviously	In other words	In particular
however	Usually	Yet
Therefore	For example	In conclusion
For instance	Similarly	but

2

but	clearly	alernatively
In short	For example	also
In other words	therefore	However
In fact	For instance	

3

Suggested key

1 of course	11 naturally
2 therefore	12 clearly
3 first of all	13 consequently
4 secondly	14 alternatively
5 in addition	15 finally
6 in summary	16 however
7 normally	
8 but	
9 as a result	
10 for example	

UNIT 6

1

Simple	**Compound**	**Complex**
1, 8	7, 11, 12	2, 3, 4, 5, 6, 9, 10

2

<u>As</u> we are changing the current reporting process, we must keep a clear record of the number of products <u>which</u> we have renewed. This will enable us to monitor our progress more closely. So, <u>when</u> the new version of the XYZ Technical Production Management software is installed, we will be able to maintain this information directly within the database. <u>After</u> all technical reports have been created within the database, we will be able to analyse data directly, <u>which</u> will eliminate the need to request this information from Application Groups via surveys, <u>as</u> it is done today.

The new technical solution will provide us with global visibility on products <u>so that</u> we can see the specific renovations <u>that</u> we have planned. The quality of the database is, of course, dependent upon the quality of the data <u>which</u> has been entered by the Application Groups. Data must be reliable and credible <u>so that</u> it can support analyses within the organisation. It must also allow, communication to external partners, <u>when</u> this is relevant. It is, therefore, critical that Application Groups enter and maintain correct data.

3

Suggested key

1 and	7 as	13 and
2 when	8 and	14 so that
3 Although	9 and	15 which
4 and	10 As	16 and
5 who	11 When	17 that
6 where	12 that	18 that

UNIT 7

Suggested answers

	1	2	3
Formal			x
Informal	x		
Distanced			
Personal	x	x	
Precise		x	x
Vague	x		
Complex			x
Simple/straightforward	x	x	
Direct			x
Indirect			
Emotional	x	x	
Neutral			x
Encouraging	x	x	
Assertive			x
Task-oriented		x	
Relationship-oriented	x		

UNIT 8

1

1 b
2 d
3 i
4 c
5 e
6 a
7 j
8 f
9 h
10 g

2

See you next week.	*Informal*
Please …	*Direct*
It is good that it will be possible for you to …	*Neutral*
Secondly we are going to …	*Relationship-oriented*
Call me if you need any help.	*Simple*
Make sure that you …	*Assertive*
We expect to see around 50 participants at the conference.	*Vague*
I am writing in connection with the last email that you sent.	*Personal*
I am looking forward to seeing you on 17 October.	*Formal*
I would appreciate it if you could …	*Indirect*
I am very pleased that you can …	*Emotional*
The next stage of the process is to …	*Task-oriented*
Don't hesitate to let me know if I can be of further assistance.	*Complex*
I believe that we should …	*Encouraging*
48 people have indicated that they will attend the forum.	*Precise*
Reference is made to your last email.	*Distanced*

3

Dear Dominic

I am writing to inform you that we are currently organising a training session on virtual project management. I would like to find a suitable date next week. Please could you let me know if Tuesday at 16.00 CET is possible for you? If so, it'll give everyone a chance to participate. We plan to schedule a conference call to bring all the project members together. Please let me know if you require any technical support.

I hope that you can join us. I look forward to your response.

Regards
Jamie

4

Dear Nick

Thanks for your email and your offer of IT support for our organisation.

I was very impressed by the range of services you offer. These do, indeed, match our requirements.

However, unfortunately at present we can't increase our spending on IT services so we won't be able to take you up on that generous introductory offer. For the future, we will monitor the situation and if things change, I will definitely contact you.

Thanks again for contacting us.

Regards
Pavel Stokowicz

UNIT 9

1

This has been a strong year of recovery, as we continued to focus on the implementation of the plans outlined last year. C
Our performance over the last year has increased confidence among customers, colleagues, and shareholders. S
The key to recovery is to increase sales. S
We are on track to hit our target of £256.2 million. S
As we move forward, we expect to see financial rewards to shareholders arising from improved sales performance and our continued focus on cost reductions. C

In March, we completed a major refinancing. S
This provided cost effective long-term finance by recognising the value in our property portfolio. C
At the same time we retain ownership of these valuable assets. S

At our AGM in July, we will be proposing a new incentive framework for arrangements to be put in place over the next ten years. C
This will build on last year's plan, applying to around 1,000 senior managers in order to retain and motivate key talent. C

The many activities that have taken place this year give encouraging signs that our recovery plan is well on course. C
Once again there has been great change for everyone. S
However, there is a real sense now around the business that the company has renewed enthusiasm and ambition. C
This view is also being echoed by many stakeholders and I would like to thank them, as I did last year, for their continued support and the part they are playing in our recovery plan. C

2

Suggested answer

Hello Martin

Thank you for your email. I am writing to confirm the details of our meeting, which will take place on 25 April from 14.00–16.00 in Room 405.

At the meeting, John and Sarah will present the current status of the project. We would like you to prepare a short presentation about the project resources for the future. The meeting room is equipped with a laptop and LCD projector so you can bring your presentation on a memory stick. Please let me know if you need any further support.

In other news, Louise Devallois is joining the team as a new project member and will be at our meeting next week. She joined the company six months ago with a background in packaging. She has considerable international experience, which will be very important for us in the future.

I look forward to seeing you on 25 April.

Regards
Bernard de Haas

3

Suggested answer

It is the policy of our company to take all reasonable steps to ensure the health and safety at work of all employees. In particular, the company will take all necessary steps to implement the policy by:

- providing a safe working environment
- monitoring safe working practices

for all employees. These steps are especially important for those whose activities are carried out in the production area where there is a greater risk of injury as a result of the industrial processes which are central to our operations.

The attention of all employees is drawn to the safety rules and procedures. These are displayed:

- throughout the production area
- in other locations on the company premises

Employees should be aware that disciplinary action, involving warning, suspension, and even dismissal (in serious cases), will be taken against any employee who is found to have violated these rules and procedures either intentionally or negligently.

As part of the continuous focus on health and safety, the company will consult with all employees periodically (and not less than twice per year) to check what additional measures might be taken to increase awareness of health and safety issues. These may include the use of:

- newsletters
- bulletins
- posters

The objective is to ensure that all necessary measures are taken to make our health and safety policy effective and to reduce the risk of injury to employees and contractors.

The company will consult with the employee representatives periodically (and not less than four times per year) to take whatever measures may be necessary to ensure:

- proper training
- supervision
- instructions

of all employees in matters relating to their health and safety. All employees therefore have the right both to be informed about existing and new measures as well as to be trained to deal with events which could lead to injury.

UNIT 10

1

Greeting	**Introduction**	**Reference**
4, 9, 12	1, 6, 15	7, 10, 13
Purpose	**Social opening**	
2, 5, 14	3, 8, 11	

2

1 d	4 b	7 g
2 h	5 a	8 c
3 f	6 i	9 e

3

Suggested key

Dear Ms Shorter
I recently read your advertisement in the Spottisberg Standard for a laboratory assistant to work in your research department …

Dear Mr Brackley
Thank you for your email about the laboratory assistant position to work in our research department. *I am writing now to invite you* for interview on …

Dear Ms Shorter
With reference to your last email, I would like to confirm that the date proposed is fine for me.

Dear Mr Brackley
Thank you for coming for interview yesterday. *We regret to inform you* that you have not been successful on this occasion. We felt that …

Dear Ms Shorter
I was sorry to read that I have not been chosen for the position of research assistant. Thank you for letting me know

UNIT 11

1

1 c	4 i	7 b
2 e	5 f	8 d
3 a	6 h	9 g

2

1 If you're interested, I would be happy to …
2 Please find attached …
3 Could you please explain …
4 It is very important that …
5 You will be delighted to hear that …
6 I am now in a position to confirm …
7 I am very sorry that you are unable to …
8 I'd like to draw your attention to …
9 I would very much like to …

3

Suggested key

1 **[Confirming]**
I am now in a position to confirm
2 **[Requesting]**
I would appreciate it if you could
3 **[Expressing urgency or necessity]**
It is very important that
4 **[Giving bad news]**
I'm afraid that
5 **[Refusing a request]**
Unfortunately, we are unable to
6 **[Reminding or highlighting]**
I'd like to draw your attention to
7 **[Making suggestions]**
We strongly recommend that
8 **[Providing documentation]**
Please find attached

4

Suggested key

1 I am now in a position to confirm that a budget has been agreed.
2 It is unlikely that we will be able to fulfil all requirements without exceeding this budget.
3 It is very important that everyone responds to this memo.
4 I'm afraid that all training will need to be done on our premises.
5 If you wish, I would be happy to discuss individual requests with any of you.

UNIT 12

1

Next steps	Pre-close 1: Offering further assistance	Pre-close 2: Friendly sign-off
4, 9, 11	1, 12, 15	2, 6, 13

Pre-close 3: Final thanks	Farewell
3, 7, 10	5, 8, 14

2

1. Recruitment
It was noted that 22 new positions had been created and a recruitment drive was under way. There was still some difficulty in bringing people into the posts, due to the time taken for pre-employment investigations. *(c) DB to check if this could be reduced. (g) DB to report back at next meeting.*

2. Turnover
Has gone down by 3% – a reflection of the insecurity in employment market. *(b) AF to monitor the position and report back at next meeting.*

3. Sickness
Absence remains at 6%. This is considered too high. *(i) RP to design a questionnaire to find out more about reasons for absence. (e) Deadline for questionnaire design: 30 September.*

4. Staff development
IB reported on successful Away Day for senior staff. It was recommended that another Away Day be timetabled for next spring. *(f) HM agreed to contact local training organisations to get ideas for themes. (d) HM to circulate info by 1 December.*

5. Christmas party
It was suggested that significant savings could be

made by holding the Christmas party in the office. This would allow more of the reduced budget to be spent on catering and entertainment. *(h) AF to contact party planners to investigate financial and practical logistics. (j) The results to be circulated by 1 September. (a) A decision to be taken at the next meeting.*

UNIT 13

1

1 Combined simple sentences to create a longer, more coherent sentence
2 Created a bulleted list which is easier to understand and to remember
3 Divided long complex sentence into two sentences
4 Split a very long paragraph into two separate paragraphs

2

Today, the growth of affordable technology has made business opportunities accessible to almost anyone with a computer and a connection to the Internet. In the past, opening a business was a huge commitment in terms of finances and risk. Traditional business owners typically had to give up their jobs, negotiate bank loans, and sign leases before they even generated a single penny of turnover. So, it is not surprising that 95% of them faced bankruptcy within five years. Today, business opportunities are available to anyone with ambition who is willing to put in the time and effort to learn about the world of e-commerce. Best of all, you can establish an e-commerce business with minimal funds and very little risk.

The first step to creating your own e-commerce business is to find your niche. You can do this by examining your hobbies and interests for potential business ideas; alternatively you can open a business that is similar to your current job, where you have insider knowledge. Now that you have a few business ideas, it is time to investigate the demand. If you plan to sell to the general public, you'll want to find out how many people are looking for your products or services. Next, find out your would-be competitors. Check their websites and spend some time exploring each one to get an idea of what you are up against.

In order to conduct business, you will need to establish a business entity and go through the various formalities of registration. When you are registered as a legitimate business owner, it is time to open a business bank account. After that, you can start creating your website. One of the keys to successful e-commerce businesses is a professional website. Remember that your website is the first and often the only impression your visitors will have of your business.

3

Suggested key

Dear Mr Johnson,

I am writing to apply for the assistant position advertised in the Evening Post. As requested I am enclosing my résumé. As you will see, I am currently working as an assistant at Burgil's HQ.

After obtaining a commercial diploma in 2000, I worked for 4 years as HR administrative assistant for a local food company. During that time I spent 2 months in Barcelona learning Spanish. Upon my return, I joined AFV's HR Department as 'on-the-job training' administrative assistant. My main tasks were the organisation of specific training for the company's technical personnel worldwide, as well as organising language classes for all AFV's employees. Four years later, I joined the Zone Americas HR team, where I worked on transfers to the markets and was responsible for welcoming expatriates to the head office.

During the next 7 years, I worked for the Productivity Team as the assistant to a team of 60 people. I was also given the opportunity to work for 5 months at AFV's Portugal Head Office, where I worked as an assistant to the Public Relation Manager. During the last few years, I have also developed my organisational skills, in particular by organising two workshops per year with about 100 participants.

Throughout my past jobs, I have developed my international skills. Thanks to the diversity of nationalities, I have also improved my language skills. I am bilingual in French and Italian, fluent in Spanish and Portuguese and have a good working knowledge of English.

Please feel free to contact me if you have any questions regarding my application.

I look forward to hearing from you.

Élise Boulanger

UNIT 14

1

Turnover

Our revenue has continued to grow for the 9th consecutive year. Although sales have only achieved growth of 1%, this is still an excellent achievement considering the world economy during this period.

Operating costs

We have focused on our costs this year and have chosen to be quite defensive. Our targets have been to:

- reduce hiring
- re-engineer our products
- refocus our marketing efforts
- drive our cost base down.

The difficult times have made this necessary and our overall performance has been improved by our new finance team.

Research and development

We continue to invest in the quality and design of our products. We believe continued investment in this area is fundamental for two reasons:

1 To continue the growth of the business
2 To create new products for the future

Environmental policy

The company as a whole continues to look for ways to develop our policy. It is our objective to improve our performance by focusing on:

- better waste treatment
- more efficient energy use
- improved indoor air quality

Future outlook for the business

Our strategy remains the same: to grow the company internationally. This year has seen the most difficult period for the UK and world economy in living memory. On balance this has done us no harm. This alone makes us very optimistic for the future. Given that we have survived the last twelve months, we should be well placed to for any future recovery.

Main uncertainties

The management of the business and the nature of the company's strategy are subject to a number of risks. The directors have set out the principal risks facing the business. These are:

- continued economic downturn
- high proportion of fixed costs
- out-of-date products
- fluctuations in currency exchange rates

People

We have a very dedicated team that is focused on creating the best possible service we can provide. I would like to thank them all for the hard work and commitment over the past year.

2

Suggested key

New Finance Opportunities[1]

A recent report by the Chicago Institute of Bankers, entitled *New Developments in Developing Country Financing*[2] has refocused attention on *mashwa-hattan*[3], or micro-financing, as it is better known to us. This publication, part of the *New Developments in Global Financing*[4] series, has become a standard work for economists wishing to find out about key issues around the world. The authors of the current work state emphatically that they do **not**[5] want to promote mashwa-hattan[6] as the sole way of motivating grass-roots entrepreneurs. However, they **do**[7] say that mashwa-hattan has created not only an alternative method of financing, but also a new spirit of independence amongst many poorer people, in significant increases in *per capita*[8] income among the rural population. A recent article in the *Times of Rotaronga*[9] pointed to real progress in the rural economy since its introduction. In a recent statement Afran Segozzi, the Minister for Rural Affairs, welcomed these new initiatives, saying that they had made a positive contribution to *finifranga*[10], the Rotarongan term for the rural economy.

Key to changes

1 Underlining or bold for heading
2 Italics for title of report
3 Italics for first use of foreign words in text
4 Italics for title of publication
5 Bold for important point
6 The second use of mashwa-hattan is not italicised
7 Bold for important point
8 Italics for loan words
9 Italics for title of newspaper
10 Italics for first use of foreign words in text

UNIT 15

1

Model answer

To: All staff
From: Jana Lipsky
Re: End-of-year party

I am writing in connection with our end-of-year party. This year there has been a suggestion that we give the money to a children's home, where it could be used to buy presents for the children. As there is not enough money for both the party and the children's home, we need to make a decision on this matter.

Please consider the following points:

The party is:

- a good opportunity for socialising and building relationships between the staff
- expensive

The children at the children's home:

- have very little and would appreciate some additional money for presents

Please let me know by 25 October whether you think we should:

1 continue with the party

2 give the money to the children's home.

Please also feel free to propose another alternative.

2

Model answer

To: IT staff
From: Andreas Olander
Re: Dress code for IT staff

I have received a number of comments from colleagues about the casual clothes worn by some of the IT staff. As you know, there is no official policy on work clothes in the company. However, normally male employees wear ties and jackets; female employees smart dresses, skirts, or trousers.

There are two key concerns:

1 The casual clothes worn in IT are causing bad feeling among other staff from other departments, who feel these clothes are inappropriate

2 The casual clothes create a poor image with visiting customers and clients

I would therefore like to propose that for now everyone in IT wears formal clothes at work. We can then discuss this matter at next month's departmental meeting and reach agreement for everyone in IT.

3

Suggested key

Minutes of staff committee held on 3 April 2011

Present: AB, JC, VD, FK, JL, FY
Apologies: MN

1 Communication in meetings

AB raised the following questions:

1 Are there too many meetings?

2 Are meetings run efficiently?

The meeting agreed to:

1 review the number of meetings

2 streamline the procedures for meeting.

AB will propose a reduced schedule of meetings for next year

JC will organise training in effective meetings.

Both actions are to be completed by May 2011.

2 Foreign travel

JL requested:

1 special compensation for weekends away

2 family support

3 intercultural training

The meeting agreed that:

1 VD will review current payments and report back at the next meeting

2 FK will investigate whether this is affordable and report back at the next meeting

3 JL will organise intercultural training by May 2011

3 New computer system

FY reported on the following problems:

1 more staff training needed

2 system very slow sometimes

The meeting agreed that:

FY will arrange a meeting with the computer system provider asap to identify solutions

UNIT 16

1

1 Regarding your recent enquiry, we are pleased to inform you that the goods are now in stock and will be mailed out to **you** later today.
2 **According to** our records, we have not received payment of our invoice dated 11 September.
3 Our payment terms clearly state that payment is due within 30 days. Payment should therefore have been received by 12 October.
4 I am writing to **confirm the details** of our next meeting, which will take place on 15 October at 14.00.
5 Could you please provide us with more **information** about your requirements. We will then be able to respond in more detail.
6 Could you please explain more precisely what you mean **by** 'unexpected delay to our delivery'?
7 I **regret to inform you** that the goods you ordered will not be in stock until next month.
8 **If I hear** nothing to the contrary, I shall assume that these terms are acceptable to you.
9 We hope that you will have no objections to **changing** the delivery address.
10 I suggest **postponing/that we postpone** the meeting until next month so that we can be sure that more of the project team will be available.
11 We would like to move forward with arranging a meeting. Therefore could you please get back to me **as soon as possible**.
12 I can absolutely assure you that the information will be treated in the strictest **confidence**.
13 **It is unlikely that we will have/We are unlikely to have** all the necessary information in time for the next meeting. Therefore I suggest we postpone the discussion till February.
14 I would like to congratulate you **on** passing the exam and wish you every success in your new position.
15 Do not hesitate to contact us if you have any further **questions**.
16 I look forward to **hearing** from you as soon as you have read through the report.

2

Model answer

Dear Mr Harrison

I would like to apply for the HR assistant position which was advertised on your website.

I have two years' experience as an intern in an international company in the food industry, where I worked in the central HR team. This has enabled me to develop know-how in recruitment and training and development. In addition, I am currently supporting a company-wide project to investigate the effectiveness of assessment centres.

I am pragmatic, dynamic, and independent. I also have a strong sense of creativity and have good organisational skills. Although I am familiar with some office software, I am keen to learn to use other HR software tools. I therefore believe that I would be an asset to your organisation. Furthermore, the assistant position would provide me with the ideal opportunity to develop my skills.

I would be delighted if you would like to meet me to discuss if my qualifications match the requirements for the position.

I have enclosed my résumé for your review and hope that you will find it of interest.

I look forward to speaking to you.

Yours sincerely

Claire Martinez

UNIT 18

1

Report section	Report element
1 Title page	c, j
2 Table of contents (or TOC)	f
3 Executive summary	i
4 Introduction/Background	d
5 Main body	a, (b), k
6 Conclusions	e
7 Recommendations	g
8 Appendices	b, h, (k)

Note: 'Detailed evidence' and 'detailed data' could go in either the main body or the appendices, depending on the length of the report.

2

Report stage	Report task
1 Preparing	d, k, h
2 Writing the first draft	b, e, j
3 Editing and producing the final version	a, c, f, g, i, l

UNIT 19

1

a	3	e	1	i	3	m	3
b	2	f	3	j	2	n	1
c	3	g	3	k	3	o	3
d	2	h	1	l	1		

2

Date: Time: Place:	Present:		Apologies for absence: *PB*	
Discussion at the meeting		**Required follow-up after the meeting**		
Agenda item	Discussion	Action (WHAT)	Person responsible (WHO)	Timeframe/ Deadline (WHEN)
1. Matters arising: *Additional office space*	*Resolved*			
2. *Staff Recruitment*	*3 in favour of recruiting new trainee.*	*Prep job spec.*	*John*	*Circulate by 15 June*
AOB: *Project planning software*				
Next Meeting: Date: ~~*4 July*~~ *11 July* Time: *9 a.m.* Place: *Boardroom*				